Helmuth Rilling

Johann Sebastian Bach's
B-Minor Mass

Translated by
Gordon Paine

Foreword by
Howard S. Swan

Prestige Publications, Inc.
Princeton, New Jersey 08540

© 1984 Prestige Publications, Inc.
International Copyright Secured. All Rights Reserved.
Printed in the United States of America.
Library of Congress Catalog Card Number: 84-60301
ISBN Number: 0-911009-05-1

.

To
Peter Kreyssig

FOREWORD

Of the many European choral conductors who make occasional visits to the United States, perhaps none has had more influence on American conductors than Helmuth Rilling. For more than a decade, he has taught master classes in the United States. His recordings, particularly those of J.S. Bach's compositions, are known and studied by musicians throughout America, and his demonstration-lectures were a high point of the 1977 convention of the American Choral Directors Association. Finally, the tours of Rilling's *Gächinger Kantorei* have provided listeners with examples of the interpretive principles that this distinguished musician has used to such great advantage.

Five years ago Helmuth Rilling published his guide to the performance of Bach's *St. Matthew Passion*. In this volume the author with consummate skill combined aspects of analysis with a suggested treatment of practical problems of interpretation, performance practice, and choral sound. In preparing this second manual on Bach's *B-Minor Mass*, Rilling has followed the same general plan, but has given more prominence to analytical investigation of the work itself. Each movement is studied in terms of its text, theological implications, and musical form and structure. Each section concludes with a thoughtful statement detailing the influence of these compositional factors upon the necessary technical and interpretive procedures to be used in rehearsal and performance. These include a discussion of suitable phrasing and articulation, the balancing of the choral and instrumental forces, the ways to secure a clarity of texture, the treatment of dynamics and diction, and the criteria to be used for the choice of a proper tempo.

Some of Rilling's observations will be of special interest to readers of his text. There are sensible and practical comments on Bach's use of symbolism. The present generation of choral conductors will be impressed with the number of times that the author stresses the necessity for Bach's musical phrases always *to move*. Such movement must be accompanied by a rhythmic vitality and a tonal intensity that preclude placid, meaningless, and dull performance. Bach's "borrowings" from earlier compositions not only demonstrate his amazing ability to rework and recreate; they also present problems and opportunities for an intelligent interpretation. Rilling gives a logical explanation for Bach's grouping of the movements contained in the *GLORIA* and *SYMBOLUM NICENUM* (*CREDO*). In the latter it is particularly significant that the CRUCIFIXUS becomes the central point and focus for the entire CREDO. With the use of many musical and textual illustrations, Rilling indicates that the conductor who performs this Mass must understand Bach's theology. For example, the opening four-bar *Kyrie* "does not primarily emphasize the prayer for mercy. Rather, in its homophonic bringing together of all forces, it expresses the declaration of Christian belief that *God is the Lord*." Another example follows a detailed discussion of the many musical means by which Bach ties together the first two movements of the *SYMBOLUM NICENUM*. Rilling explores *why* Bach wished to do so: "Bach was entirely conscious of the inseparability of the components of the sentence *Credo in unum Deum, Patrem omnipotentem, factorem coeli et terrae, visibilium omnium et invisibilium*. Since, despite the unity of this text, he attempted to set it in two different forms and styles, and to connect the two resulting movements as intimately as possible, it seems that he wished to present the CREDO IN UNUM DEUM as dogma, free from all subjective elements. When that text is accepted as reality in the PATREM OMNIPOTENTEM, it turns into a glorification of God that extends 'to the ends of the earth.'" There are many theological implications such as these scattered throughout the book.

Helmuth Rilling's treatise on the *B-Minor Mass* is an important and helpful contribution to those who wish to expand their understanding of the compositonal genius of J.S. Bach. Those in the English-speaking world will be grateful to Professor Gordon Paine of California State University, Fullerton, who is responsible for a remarkably lucid and comprehensive translation from the original German.

Howard S. Swan
Newport Beach, California

TRANSLATOR'S NOTE

In several ways, this first English edition of Helmuth Rilling's discussion of the B-Minor Mass is more of a revision than just a translation. Professor Rilling has taken this opportunity to rewrite certain portions of the original German text (Hänssler Verlag, 1979), both adding and deleting material. Too, it has been possible to clarify some musical examples and to correct mistakes that appeared in the German edition.

The translator is indebted to Professor Rilling for his helpful critiques of the English text.

Gordon Paine
Fullerton, California

CONTENTS

PREFACE

Johann Sebastian Bach's *B-Minor Mass* occupies a special place in his life's work. It belongs to the group of works that he sorted through, revised, and assembled into collections in the final years of his life. Whereas at that time he merely corrected those works already completed—the *St. Matthew Passion*, for example—Bach formulated his Mass from the ground up. Though he was able to make use of the *KYRIE* and *GLORIA* of 1733 and the *SANCTUS* of 1724, the remaining sections of the Mass had to be newly conceived.

For some of the new movements Bach needed, he availed himself of works from earlier creative periods and transformed them into Mass movements. Since, despite his consummate parody technique, he did not take all of the Mass movements from previously existing works, the newly composed portions (CREDO IN UNUM DEUM, ET IN UNUM DOMINUM, ET INCARNATUS EST, ET IN SPIRITUM SANCTUM, and CONFITEOR UNUM BAPTISMA) assume a special significance: they are in all probability Bach's last compositions to sacred texts.

The motivation behind the composition of the *B-Minor Mass* differed from that of all of Bach's other sacred works. He composed all of the cantatas and motets, as well as the two Passions, for a single, specific performance that he conducted himself. But of all the sections of the *B-Minor Mass*, such performance can be proven only for the *SANCTUS*. It is possible that there was also a performance of the *KYRIE* and *GLORIA* in Dresden, though this cannot be documented. Bach probably never heard the remaining movements of the Mass (*SYMBOLUM NICENUM, OSANNA, BENEDICTUS, AGNUS DEI*, and *DONA NOBIS PACEM*).

Thus, Bach's *B-Minor Mass* is the summation and culmination of his life's work. With the supreme command of vocal and instrumental compositional techniques that he had developed over his lifetime and the absence of the urgency of an impending performance, Bach was prepared to come face to face with the awesome task of dealing with the central tenets of the Christian faith.

The writings of many other authors deal with questions regarding the history and criticism of the original sources, the genesis of the work and the possibility of its performance in Bach's lifetime, the collective unity of the sections of the Mass, problems of performance practice, the quality of practical editions, and other aspects of the work. I will therefore not deal with these subjects here. For basic information, I am above all indebted to the fundamental, primary research of Georg von Dadelsen.[1] In addition, Walter Blankenburg's *Einführung in H-moll Messe*[2] was most helpful in its collation of material on the Mass from secondary sources.

It is not my purpose in my discussion of individual aspects of the *B-Minor Mass* to engage in judgemental comparison of, or to duplicate the work of, previous writers. I am far more interested in Bach's Mass itself. In this study I will analyze Bach's Mass and explore its overall architecture, the structure of its various sections, the form of the individual movements, and the structure of the thematic and motivic materials. Possible ways of interpreting both details and larger relationships within the Mass will arise from these structural-analytical investigations.

These efforts at interpretation have as their basis our modern, secularized way of looking at music. But though this approach to musical understanding permits us to comprehend and appreciate the aesthetic dimension of Bach's music, it provides little access to the theological substance of his work, which is at least as important. I will therefore purposely address this subject as well.

In my analyses I will develop my interpretations from the musical facts themselves. I do not intend to discuss aspects of the work that seem to me to have no bearing on the architectural and structural elements of the piece, or to be of little importance in that regard (number symbolism, for example). The aggregate of the thoughts and observations presented necessarily has implications for the shaping of the work in performance (in italic print at the end of each section). Nevertheless, I will address only the basic elements of these implications, and not their details.

Helmuth Rilling

KYRIE

Bach composed the *KYRIE*—with its tripartite textual division *Kyrie eleison-Christe eleison-Kyrie eleison*—in three extensive movements. The fact that so few words are treated so extensively assigns to the *KYRIE* a fundamental significance within the complete Mass. Bach omitted the trumpets and timpani from the orchestration of the work as a whole and used the relatively soft oboes d'amore instead of regular oboes. With this orchestration and the inclusion of the chorus, he formulated the two outer movements as tuttis. Though the middle section — the CHRISTE ELEISON — is for soloists, it also has the character of a piece for larger ensemble—two voices engage in dialogue with a two-part instrumental setting.

KYRIE ELEISON I

In the first movement of the *KYRIE,* Bach sets the text *Kyrie eleison* (Lord, have mercy) in two different ways. He begins with a chordal introduction, which is followed by a large-scale fugue. This procedure is quite striking, since Bach interprets a single text with the use of different musical material at only one other place in the Mass, the ET EXPECTO. In addition, it is interesting to observe that Bach begins none of his other large, oratorio-like works with block chords and a simultaneous choral-orchestral tutti. Rather, he always constructs the introductory movements by gradual development.

These two characteristics explain the special expressive quality of the opening bars to the *KYRIE.* Bach was not satisfied to begin the Mass with a fugue, a form with its own inherent evolution of the thematic material and reflective interpretation of the text. He places objectivity before diversity, beginning with four measures (ex. 1) that possess the character of a banner headline, not just for the *KYRIE,* but for the entire Mass. This short *Kyrie*—the threefold nature of which was perhaps intended to relate to the three persons of the Trinity, God the Father, God the Son, and God the Holy Spirit—does not primarily emphasize the prayer for mercy. Rather, in its homophonic bringing together of all forces, it expresses the declaration of Christian belief that *God is the Lord.* Inherent in this confession of God's supremacy is also the concept of man's subordination to God; to this end, the appeal for mercy (*eleison*) sounds twice, in two voices at a time, in the initial three bars. When this word is taken up by all parts on the upbeat to bar 4, and the harmonic tension built up in the previous measures is released in intensity of sound and rhythm (the latter created primarily by the violins) with a cadence on the dominant, the majestic conclusion renews the credo that God guarantees His mercy.

Ex. 1

For the shaping of the introductory measures in performance, any excessive expressiveness or hectic agitation must be deliberately avoided. In the first two measures, the anacruses of three rising eighth notes on the word *eleison* in the two soprano parts must build a definite tension to the downbeat of the following measure, just as the first three measures must build tension to the fourth. The intensity of the last measure—brought about largely by the sixteenth-note motion—must be clearly audible, particularly in the first violin.

3

The subject of the fugue that begins now (ex. 2)

Ex. 2

is derived from the bass line of the opening bars by chromatic alteration. In contrast to the first four bars, however, the emphasis is not on the word *kyrie*, but rather, on the melisma to which the word *eleison* is set.

The fugue subject consists of four structural components. The first is the beginning of the subject—the repeated notes on the word *kyrie*—the firm, dotted rhythm of which is a diminution of the predominant rhythm of the opening measures. The second structural component is the chromatically ascending line B - C sharp^1 - D^1 - D sharp^1 - E^1, followed by the answering downward motion in which C natural and A sharp are added to the chromatic scale. Here, for the first time in the Mass, Bach uses chromatic material, with its characteristic, intense expressive value: every pitch between A sharp and E^1 is employed. Perhaps Bach conceived this setting of the word *eleison* symbolically: just as the sinner asking God's mercy (*eleison*) cannot escape judgement, no pitches between A sharp and E^1 escape use in this portion of the subject. The third structural component is the unexpected, rather startling leap of a seventh that follows. This leap forces the up to this point seemingly resigned, falling line back into the primary key and gives immediate expressive impact to the repeat of the word *kyrie*. The fourth element of the fugue subject is the falling-half-step motive G - F sharp, consisting of two eighth notes. When employed instrumentally, the motive is slurred, giving stress to the first note. This motive is a basic symbol in Bach's musical language. He employed it in his earliest extant cantata, *Aus der Tiefe rufe ich* (BWV 131: Out of the Depths I Cry) in conjunction with the word *Flehen* ("pleading") (ex. 3).

Ex. 3

The same symbol is used in many ways, with similar expression, throughout Bach's works. We find it, for example, in a passage (ex. 4) from the motet *Der Geist hilft unsrer Schwachheit auf* (BWV 226: The Spirit Helps Our Weakness), in which the motive is associated with the word *Seufzen* ("sighs").

Ex. 4

These examples characterize well the expressive quality of the motive as it is used in the fugue subject of the KYRIE ELEISON I: it formulates the urgency and insistence of the prayer for God's mercy.

Throughout the entire fugue, Bach uses but one countermotive in combination with the beginning of the principal motive (ex. 5). In each case, it enters a quarter note after the beginning of the subject, is held as a syncopation, then moves down a half step (in contrary motion to the contour of the main subject), and returns immediately to the initial pitch. In contrast with other of Bach's fugues, he does not extend this countermotive into a counter-subject, as would be expected in strict counterpoint. Rather, he uses a variety of different extensions so that the fugue subject is always dominant — even when it is treated fragmentarily, with free development of its eight-note motion.

Ex. 5

On the other hand, there are eight episodes (mm. 15-18, 35-36, 42-43, 58-61, 86-87, 93-96, 99/3-101, and 112-115) that are distinguished by the presence of independent motives and the absence of further development of the motives from the main subject. For example, in the opening bars to the fourth of these episodes (ex. 6), the motive in the two soprano parts that begins on the pickup to beat three is imitated canonically a quarter note later in the woodwinds and the two violin parts. In addition, three independent motives—in the bass, continuo, and the tenor and alto, respectively—are adhered to without alteration. Only the viola has a filler part.

Ex. 6

It is the peculiar nature of several of these episodes that they possess no tendency toward development, unlike the linear, development-oriented sections characterized by the presence of the fugue subject. In the course of the self-evolving fugue, these episodes assume the function of reflective pauses.

The 122-measure fugue is structured in two large-scale choral development sections (mm. 30-72 and 81-126), each of which is preceded by an instrumental introduction. The use of restrained dynamics at the beginning of the fugue is suggested by Bach's choice of instrumentation: the relatively soft woodwinds, which play in low tessitura and dominate the strings, which recede into the background. That Bach also desired restrained dynamics in the first choral development up to m. 45, is clear from the use of two oboes d'amore. Only when the instruments return to playing *colla voce* does a development begin (mm. 45-52) that, along with the modulations that move the setting into a higher range, generates intensification. After the episode that cuts short this development and pauses reflectively (mm. 58-60), come the transitional measures (mm. 61-64, ex. 7) to the last entrance of the subject in the first part of the fugue. These measures, built upon the sighing motive of the subject, are of exceptionally expressive quality.

Ex. 7

In the instrumental passage that follows (mm. 72/3-80), the transitions between the entries of the subject (mm. 74/4-76/1 and 78/4-81/1) are still characterized by the use of the sighing motive. The passage receives its particular expressive character from the sudden reduction of forces to just a continuo-supported oboe duet, as well as from the second entrance of the subject (m. 76), the only entrance in the entire fugue in a major key. With this reduction of forces and the major-key statement of the subject, the release of tension and the lightening of mood in this section give Bach the chance to begin the second choral development of the subject with renewed restraint.

In the second development the setting evolves from the initial, low-lying entrances of the subject in the bass and tenor. But in contrast with the first development, the beginning here is not accompanied by just the two oboes. Now the flutes and oboes play together, and the violins and violas are given obbligato parts. Even here, at the beginning, one can perceive a nascent desire on Bach's part to make the second development of the subject more intense than the first. This notion is reinforced by the fact that he now has the orchestra begin to play *colla voce* only seven bars after the choir enters, compared to fifteen-and-one-half bars in the first development. In addition, the episodes in the fugue (mm. 86-87, 93-96, and 99/3-101), which served as reflective pauses in the first development of the subject, are now less contrapuntally dense. But here they are intimately involved in the building and release of tension within the development as a whole. For example, mm. 93-96 (ex. 8) contain a two-measure intensification produced by a rising sequence and a relaxation achieved by a falling sequence.

7

Ex. 8

The section that follows this example (mm. 97-111) brings with it an almost tempestuous development which takes the setting into intense upper ranges with three statements of the subject and an upward-sequencing episode. But then Bach returns to the model of the first development and concludes the movement—after a once-again contrapuntal episode and transitional measures characterized by the sighing motive—with a statement of the subject in the bass.

The shaping of the extensive KYRIE ELEISON I fugue must be consistent with the structure of the movement, as discussed above. In the forming of the subject, the expressive value of the ascending seventh must not be diminished by a breath before the word kyrie. *Too, there must be a linear development to this climactic top note. It is important to the ebb and flow of tension within the movement that the dynamics underscore the intensification created by the structure. The episodes in the first development should be relaxed; those of the second development should enter much more into the overall intensification.*

Another possibility for the building of tension within the fugue lies in the thoughtful consideration of tempo. This movement—which Bach marked "largo" and to which he allocated so much space within his setting of the Mass text—must begin very slowly, so that with the gradual development of the thematic material, sufficient time and tranquility are allowed for unhurried meditation and reflection on the meaning of the words kyrie eleison. *In the second half of the fugue, however, a tempo that presses forward to climaxes might well be a possibility, in order to emphasize the expressive components of the subject and to provide a more intense and vital contrast to the initial restraint and reflectivity.*

CHRISTE ELEISON

Bach sets the CHRISTE ELEISON, like the ET IN UNUM DOMINUM later in the Mass, as a vocal duet—perhaps symbolic of Christ, the second person of the Trinity, who is addressed in the texts of both movements. The musical setting of the CHRISTE ELEISON stands in stark contrast to the preceding KYRIE ELEISON I fugue. From the beginning, the instrumental introduction acquires freshness and vitality from the almost-continuous sixteenth-note movement in the violins and from the walking eighths in the continuo. This motion is itself enriched rhythmically by syncopated entrances and tied eighths (ex. 9). The setting also acquires brilliance from the change to the major key and gains firmness and strength from the unison scoring for the two violins, which corresponds to the string unison in the continuo.

Ex. 9

Structurally, three types of composition characterize the vocal setting. It begins with a homophonic duet (ex. 10), a period of four bars in which the rhythmic variety is noteworthy: Bach uses sixteenths, sixteenth triplets, syncopations, and tied notes. A group of

Ex. 10

9

measures follows, built on vocal imitation (ex. 11). The third structural element is the

Ex. 11

complementary rhythm of the two voices, characterized by mutual alternation of sixteenth-note motion (ex. 12).

Ex. 12

When one compares the elements of construction of this movement with those of the surrounding KYRIE ELEISON settings, it becomes clear that the obvious concentration on one fixed subject in each of the KYRIE ELEISONS contrasts with the variety of themes Bach deliberately sought in the CHRISTE ELEISON. Only one motivic component of the subject of the preceding fugue resembles anything found in the CHRISTE ELEISON, i.e. the motive of two, slurred, falling eighths—Bach's symbol for sighing and pleading—which characterizes two places in the movement. In the CHRISTE ELEISON, however, the motive is rhythmically different and therefore camouflaged. In its first appearance (ex. 13), it occurs alone in each voice individually, then twice in homophony. In the second

Ex. 13

appearance of the motive, it is set homophonically only once. The special expressive content of the motive is then completely dissolved by the linear writing for both voices at the interval of a sixth (ex. 14). These observations show clearly that Bach was eager to fashion a

Ex. 14

central piece for his setting of the complete *Kyrie* text that would stand out in relief from the construction and density of the surrounding fugues by virtue of its thematic variety and rhythmic animation.

In Bach's musical representation of the meaning of the *Christe eleison* text, he deemphasizes the elements of sighing and pleading. A confident, even joyous attitude takes their place, based on the trust in God's guarantee of mercy through Christ. At the close of the vocal setting, this expressive quality is made especially clear by the pedal point in the continuo and the sharp, syncopated entrance of the violins on the high major third (ex. 15).

Ex. 15

For the shaping of the CHRISTE ELEISON, it is important to choose a tempo that is not too tranquil, in order to emphasize the vivacity of the movement. Too, the instruments must radiate intensity, and one must be aware that a string section is performing rather than just individual players. When the singers enter, the instrumental parts should be heard not as mere accompaniment. Rather, their obbligato figuration, which is thematically essential, must be clearly audible. The liveliness and diversity of the instrumental setting can be emphasized further through the use of echo effects, which might be employed for the first time in mm. 5-7, as shown in example 16.

Ex. 16

KYRIE ELEISON II

Bach wrote the *KYRIE ELEISON II* in the *stile antico*, the traditional style of sixteenth-century church music. This is in deliberate contrast to the structural variety of the CHRISTE ELEISON. As well, it is an effort to differentiate this setting from the KYRIE ELEISON I. The external signs of the *stile antico* here are the tempo indication *alla breve* and the notation of the movement in long notes, the basic pulse being the half note. The scoring likewise reflects the motet model of the Palestrina period in that, excluding the continuo, the instruments have no obbligato function, but rather play *colla parte* with the four voice parts. The voice leading also has its roots in the contrapuntal technique of Renaissance vocal music. An expansive, linear, diatonic style of writing characterizes the movement; melodic leaps occur rarely. Though Bach copies an earlier style, he does not employ the traditional model without modifying it. This can be seen clearly in the subject of the fugue; while the rising and falling of the line in the second half of the subject on the word *eleison* is a formula used frequently in the sixteenth-century motet style ("the arched phrase"), the intervallic content of the beginning of the subject is, however, of Bach's own invention. This is clear only from the underlying continuo part and its figuring.

In an abrupt change of the F-sharp-minor tonality established on the downbeat of the opening measure, Bach introduces a Neapolitan sixth-chord on beat two. The tonal order that is thus destroyed is reestablished by the subsequent modulations that gradually lead back to the tonic key (ex. 17). The similarity of this unusual beginning to the most

Ex. 17

harmonically dense point in the subject of the KYRIE ELEISON I is remarkable (ex. 18). Here too, the Neapolitan sixth-chord appears, although the modulation subsequently takes a different course.

Ex. 18

In the organization of the movement as well, Bach follows no a-priori formal scheme. Rather, he employs the fugue and uses his own logic of construction. There are four expositions of the fugue subject. It appears first in paired voices—initially in the bass and tenor, and following an episode, in the alto and soprano. In the second exposition it stands alone in the alto (m. 18), bass (m. 25), and tenor (m. 29), respectively. It is noteworthy that after the balance and tranquility of the first exposition, Bach intensifies the second in three ways.

First, he inserts into the continuo and tenor, then later into the bass and continuo, a motive of a chromatically stepwise-rising fourth (ex. 19), seen previously in the subject of the KYRIE ELEISON I fugue and later found in several movements of the *SYMBOLUM NICENUM*. At the same time, the alto (m. 17), and later the tenor (m. 22), enter on

Ex. 19

syncopations, which Bach has avoided up to this time. Finally, with the entrance of the bass on the fugue subject (m. 25), the continuo gives up its previous independence and intensifies the bass line by doubling it. The third and fourth expositions of the subject are characterized by the stretto that appears first in mm. 35-36 (ex. 20). The three paired-voice stretto

Ex. 20

entrances of the fugue subject (alto and tenor, mm. 35-36; soprano and bass, mm. 40-41 and 54-55) acquire their particular expressive value from the three choral fugatos (beginning mm. 31/3, 43/1, and 51/1) that mingle with them (ex. 21). These fugatos break up the previous strictness and austerity of structure by their unexpected syncopated entrances in high tessitura ranges. They also emphasize the structural density of the following strettos on the fugue subject.

Ex. 21

An examination of the implications of the structure for the growth and dissipation of tension within the movement leads inescapably to the conclusion that there is a gradual intensification. If one considers the movement as a whole, its placement within the *KYRIE*, and Bach's interpretation of the text within it, one must conclude that Bach used the *stile antico* in order to exclude subjective expression. With the KYRIE ELEISON II, it seems as if Bach desired to carve a niche for himself both within the age-old prayer for mercy of the Church—*Kyrie eleison*—and the history of its music. The fugue subject, with its rather objective character, seems to embody at the same time the expressiveness of the preceding movements. Its chromatic beginning reflects the intensity of the fugue subject of the KYRIE ELEISON I, its melismatic continuation embodies the relaxed mood of the CHRISTE ELEISON, and the rhythmic firmness of the half notes at the beginning of the subject possesses the affirmational character of the opening bars of the KYRIE ELEISON I. But following the expositions, Bach seems to depart immediately from the objectivity and austerity of the movement, and to break into jubilation with the high, syncopated fugato entrances of the four voices. The KYRIE ELEISON II thus acquires a new dimension and reveals what so distinguishes Bach's thinking in the composition of the various Mass movements: the ability to compose to one text while simultaneously foreshadowing the next movement—in this case, the GLORIA IN EXCELSIS DEO.

The shaping of the movement must follow the dictates of its structure. Specifically, the performers must use a decisive and weighty articulation for the chromatic intervals at the beginning of the subject and then a vocal-style, linear legato for the rest of the subject and the motives derived from it. The structural compression of the movement must be reinforced by intensity of sound at the end of the second exposition of the subject (m. 31), so that the overlapping fugato is heard as a climax. The first stretto (mm. 35-36), usually the culmination of a fugal exposition, must here be the point of departure for an intensification that culminates in the high entrances of the last fugato section (mm. 51-52) and the following citation of the subject (m. 54).

16

GLORIA

Compared to the *KYRIE*, the text of the *GLORIA* is quite lengthy. Bach divided it into eight movements.

Movement 1: GLORIA IN EXCELSIS DEO, *et in terra pax hominibus bonae voluntatis.*
Movement 2: LAUDAMUS TE, *benedicimus te, adoramus te, glorificamus te,*
Movement 3: GRATIAS AGIMUS TIBI *propter magnam gloriam tuam:*
Movement 4: DOMINE DEUS, *Rex coelestis, Deus Pater omnipotens. Domine Fili unigenite, Jesu Christe altissime; Domine Deus, Agnus Dei, Filius Patris:*
Movement 5: QUI TOLLIS PECCATA MUNDI, *miserere nobis; qui tollis peccata mundi, suscipe deprecationem nostram;*
Movement 6: QUI SEDES AD DEXTERAM PATRIS, *miserere nobis*
Movement 7: QUONIAM TU SOLUS SANCTUS, *tu solus Dominus, tu solus altissimus: Jesu Christe,*
Movement 8: CUM SANCTO SPIRITU *in gloria Dei Patris. Amen.*

The logic behind Bach's division of the text is discernible from his use of chorus in movements 1, 3, 5, and 8, and his assignment of soloists to the remaining portions of the text. The two sections of text containing the word *Gloria* (movements 1 and 3) become choral movements that frame the LAUDAMUS TE (2), a solo movement. Bach was able to carry out his plan to place the QUI TOLLIS PECCATA MUNDI (5) at the center of the *GLORIA* by making the DOMINE DEUS (4) and the QUI SEDES AD DEXTERAM PATRIS (6) into solo movements. Following these groups of three related pieces each, Bach divides the remaining text into two movements, the first (7) for vocal and instrumental soloists and the second (8) for a choral-orchestral tutti.

With the *GLORIA*, Bach completely changes his compositional style. He calls out the trumpets and timpani and exchanges the oboes d'amore for the more-powerful, regular oboes. For his compositional structure, he intentionally uses concertato technique with strongly virtuosic elements. The use of virtuosic concertato writing is quite evident in the tutti movements, which place great technical demands on both the singers and players. But it is to be seen even more in the arias, in which the soloistic, and at times, virtuosic, element in both the voices and instruments is deliberately brought to the fore. The soprano I and tenor, soprano II, alto, and bass—representatives of each of the choral voice groups—receive solo assignments with the flute, violin, oboe, and hunting horn, respectively—representatives of each of the instrumental families of the orchestra. The intentional contrast with the *KYRIE* is obvious. Bach approached the text of the *Kyrie eleison* with humility, and though he was very expressive, he restrained himself by his conservative choice of compositional techniques. He abandons this reserve with the text *Gloria in excelsis Deo* ("Glory to God in the highest") and develops every possibility of vocal and instrumental sonority within a striking concertato compositional technique.

GLORIA IN EXCELSIS DEO

For the beginning of the *GLORIA*, Bach writes a concerto setting which, in every respect, stands out in relief from the preceding KYRIE ELEISON II. Instead of F-sharp minor, Bach uses the radiant key of D major; instead of the "old" *alla breve*, the modern ⅜ meter; instead of *colla-parte* instrumentation, first a virtuosic orchestral introduction, then obbligato writing for the instruments. The choir of only four voices and the restraint of orchestration characterized by the oboes d'amore, give way to five-voice choral scoring and the brilliance of the trumpets. Motoric rhythm now dominates instead of linearity and a cantabile quality.

In contrast with the fugue subject of the preceding KYRIE ELEISON II, which was developed out of the rhythm and flow of the words, the main theme of the GLORIA IN EXCELSIS DEO, with its broken triad, is instrumentally conceived. The later setting of this GLORIA IN EXCELSIS DEO theme to text appears haphazard, confirming its instrumental origin (ex. 22).

Ex. 22

The priority Bach gives to idiomatic instrumental writing is even more obvious in a four-measure period (mm. 9-12) that he developed in the instrumental introduction from the sixteenth-note motive in the first measure (ex. 23). Its texted equivalent in the two

Ex. 23

sopranos (ex. 24) proves to be barely viable on its own; it stands in need of the fugato in the remaining voices of the choir. A final example is the eight-measure period that closes the

18

Ex. 24

instrumental introduction (mm. 17-25), a logical, fully-developed passage including a six-measure (3 × 2) sequence and a hemiolic conclusion (ex. 25). Once again, with the

Ex. 25

addition of the voices to this eight-measure period that Bach formulates twice (mm. 57-64 and mm. 93-100), the voice leading, rhythm, and text underlay appear relatively haphazard (ex. 26).

Ex. 26

The previously observed proclivity toward concerto-like writing within the eight settings that comprise the *GLORIA* is so obvious in the first part of the opening movement that it seems quite plausible that Bach adapted the GLORIA IN EXCELSIS DEO from a now-lost instrumental concerto. Nevertheless, the likelihood of an instrumental origin for the music and the playful virtuosity derived from it do not lead to a neglect of the vocal setting. Indeed, the frequent vocal variation of the instrumental periods is an imaginative enrichment of the setting. When individual voice parts break away from such strict periods (for example, the tenor in m. 53 or the alto in m. 89), the expression is an exuberant, and very musical vitality (ex. 27).

Ex. 27

In the final bars of the GLORIA IN EXCELSIS DEO, Bach takes the soprano into the extreme upper register in symbolism of the words *in excelsis* ("in the highest") (ex. 28). Then,

Ex. 28

on the words *et in terra pax* ("and on earth peace"), the absolute antithesis follows, also related to the text. Bach moves to a low register through a modulation to the subdominant (G major), changes from fast 3/4 time to calmer 4/4 movement, and reduces the scoring to just continuo-supported choir (ex. 29).

Ex. 29

The architecture of the following section is exceptionally expansive. Bach begins with lyrical restraint; in the opening bars it almost seems as if he had taken—in advance—the mood from the Pastoral Symphony of the *Christmas Oratorio* he was to compose just one year later. But with the upbeat to m. 6, the slurred-eighth-note theme rises from the bass through the middle voices until it permeates the entire setting and reaches for a climax (ex. 30)—first of all in m. 12, in which the text *hominibus bonae voluntatis* ("to men of good will") comes together homophonically in all parts following the preceding fugato development, then again in m. 19, with identical music in the instruments. The focus here is on *man —hominibus—* and the music moves and builds inexorably toward that word. The forceful-ness that finds expression in these two deliberately set intense sections and the homophonic cadences that close them, intimates that Bach wanted the words *hominibus bonae volunta-tis* interpreted not in the cheerful sense of the Christmas story ("good will toward men"), but rather, in the literal sense of the Latin text, "to men of good will."

Ex. 30

The fugue subject Bach develops out from the previous fugato motive is characterized by a relaxed mood and lightheartedness, due primarily to the dotted rhythm on the word *hominibus*. (The manuscript leaves some doubt as to whether dotted rhythm or even rhythm was intended. The contention that Bach wanted even rhythm has some independent support: when he used the same music later in Cantata 191, the rhythm was even.)

The entire first section of the fugue up to and including m. 37 retains this basic character by virtue of the treatment of the subject and the sixteenth-note-coloratura countersubject that always accompanies it, supported only by light, chordal accompaniment in both orchestra and continuo (ex. 31).

Ex. 31

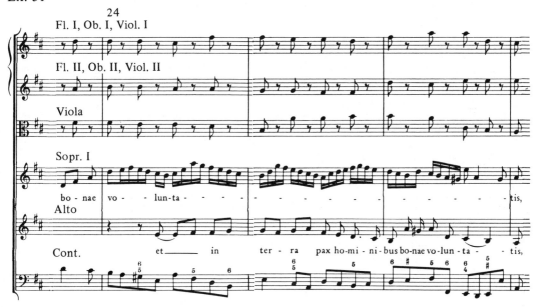

The alternation of block-like statements between the chorus and orchestra in the bars that follow (mm. 38-43) provides the transition to the second development of the fugue subject. This transition begins in m. 43, emphasized by the reentrance of the timpani. The next section of the fugue, up to m. 49, corresponds thematically to the first, but it acquires a different character from the *colla-parte* accompaniment of the orchestra. Whereas the first section was light and playful, this section is now intensified and impelled forward to the trumpet-led climax in mm. 57-59. Once again the course of the fugue is interrupted by the block-like, concertato opposition of the individual groups of the ensemble in the following measures. Then follows a compositionally essential building of intensity to the final section in which the theme is presented: Bach progressively adds to the orchestra in mm. 63-65 and then writes upward-building sequences in mm. 66-69. With the presentation of the theme in the alto, the simultaneous concertato activity of the violas, and the upward-running sixteenths in the violins that lead to the brilliant thematic entrance of the first trumpet in m. 73, the movement comes to its vigorous, triumphantly vital conclusion.

It is interesting to examine this music in detail, since it becomes apparent in the course of Bach's composition of the text *et in terra pax hominibus bonae voluntatis*, that a consciously sought transformation in the meaning of the text evolves. From the lyricism of the Christmas-eve reminiscence, the urgency of the words *hominibus bonae voluntatis*, and the relaxed and light-hearted beginning of the fugue, spans an arch leading from an understanding of the text as a prophecy of the future, to the end of the movement, where this prophetic vision appears to be triumphantly fulfilled: there *will* be peace on earth for men of good will.

There are two basic problems in the shaping of the work for performance. For the first half of the movement, the articulation of the principal theme must be identical in both the voices and instruments. Though staccato articulation is essential here, the rhythmic aspect of the music must not be overpowering. The articulation must also reinforce the linear tendency of the music, which aims toward the fifth measure. This building of tension can be achieved through dynamic differentiation.

The second problem—one of great interpretive significance—is the organization of the measures into periods and the delineation of the mutual boundaries of these periods. One way in which this can be accomplished is by emphasizing the building and relaxation of tension through dynamic variation—in mm. 9-12 and 13-16, for example. A second way is to bring to the surface the hemiola figures that close such periods by superimposing accents of the three quarter notes over the usual three-eighth-note units.

The dynamic scheme of the second half of the movement should follow the previously discussed structural intensification. The differentiation among the various affects of the text can be accomplished through articulatory variation: staccato *for the relaxed, joyous beginning of the fugue;* strong non legato *for the second development of the subject; and* marcato *for the final part of the fugue.*

LAUDAMUS TE

For the centerpiece of the triptych of movements that begins the *GLORIA*, Bach writes an aria, the uniqueness of which lies in the strongly virtuosic character of the solo parts. The setting is quite demanding for both the solo violin and the mezzo soprano with regard to playing and singing technique as well as rhythmic accuracy. Yet with the structure Bach chooses for this movement, the virtuosity one expects of both the vocal and instrumental parts never seems showy or excessive. Though many of the principles of construction of the aria are similar to those of the concerto grosso, the original "piano" indication in m. 3 shows that Bach certainly did not intend an actual solo-tutti contrast (ex. 32). The string setting

Ex. 32

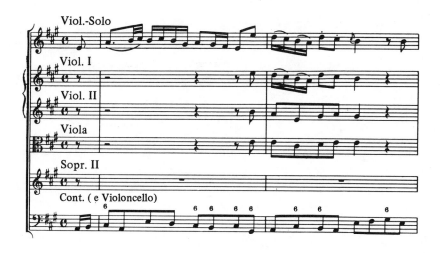

does not function merely as an accompaniment; rather, Bach gives it an obbligato role in the thematic working out of the movement. For example, in m. 18, the strings support the soprano; in mm. 19 and 20 they construct a fugato that is continued by the voice; and then in mm. 21 and 22, they join with the solo violin (ex. 33).

Ex. 33

The difficulty of the vocal figuration in the continuo-accompanied middle section (ex. 34)

Ex. 34

is similar to that of the solo violin in the purely instrumental sections (ex. 35). Nevertheless,

Ex. 35

there is no externally brilliant character in either of these cases. Even in the final measures, when the two soloists come together after their dialogue (ex. 36), great compositional subtlety characterizes the considerable technical and rhythmic demands made on the violin and mezzo soprano, respectively.

Ex. 36

Thus, between the large-scale tutti movements—the GLORIA IN EXCELSIS DEO and the GRATIAS AGIMUS TIBI—Bach places a chamber music-like setting of the four textual ideas, *Laudamus te, benedicimus te, adoramus te, glorificamus te* ("we praise You, we bless You, we worship You, we glorify You"). Beneath the concertato techniques visible on the surface, Bach writes an exceptionally delicate setting. The expression of the movement is aptly described by the text to the opening movement to cantata BWV 120, which Bach sets similarly: *Gott, man lobet dich in der Stille* ("God, man praises You in the stillness [of Zion]").

Proper tempo is critical to this piece. It must be fast enough that the natural liveliness of the opening bars is preserved, yet slow enough that the violinist can play the thirty-second-note coloraturas musically, and the mezzo soprano can confidently sing the ornamentation in m. 13.

The structure of the movement demands that the two soloists be equally balanced. One must also take notice of the often-low tessitura of the voice part. The strings should accompany with a variety of dynamics, so that all elements of the setting remain audible throughout, and the individual thematic figurations in the orchestra are clearly understood.

GRATIAS AGIMUS TIBI

This is the first movement within the *B-Minor Mass* that is certainly a reworking of a previously composed cantata movement. The adaptation is based on the choral movement *Wir danken dir, Gott, wir danken dir*, from the 1731 cantata of the same name (BWV 29). Bach may have had two reasons to choose this particular cantata movement as the basis for his new composition. First, the messages of the German text of the cantata (*Wir danken dir, Gott, wir danken dir, und verkündigen deine Wunder:* "We thank You, God; we thank You and proclaim Your wonders") and the Latin text of the Mass (*Gratias agimus tibi propter magnam gloriam tuam:* "We thank You for Your great glory") are nearly identical. Second, a contrast of style between the GRATIAS AGIMUS TIBI and the preceding, concerto-like movement, seems to have been important to Bach: in the cantata, there is also such a contrast between the choral movement and the preceding, concerto-like movement for solo organ and orchestra, which is derived from the partita in E major for solo violin, BWV 1006.

Like the KYRIE ELEISON II, this movement was conceived in the *stile antico*. Bach has the orchestra play *colla voce* with the choir and for the moment, dispenses with obbligato instrumental parts. Proceeding from the bipartite theme of the cantata model,

Bach also associated each of the two halves of the Mass text with an individualized theme (ex. 37) and worked both into the counterpoint of a freely handled double fugue.

Ex. 37

The linearity and cantabile nature of the first theme stands out in clear relief against the rhythmically stronger and more differentiated character of the second. Bach's use of the trumpets and timpani in this movement is truly remarkable. First, he has the trumpet I double the soprano part at the climaxes of two sections at the beginning of the setting (mm. 15-18 and mm. 26-29). Then, beginning at m. 31, in a brilliant extension of the *stile antico* practice—usually the instruments simply double the voices—he brings in the second trumpet, followed by the first trumpet, and finally the third trumpet and timpani, as obbligato instruments above the previously four-voice setting (ex. 38). At this point, it seems as if a halo of sound representing the glory of God (*magnam gloriam*) ascends above the earthly *gratias agimus*.

Ex. 38

28

In the shaping of the fugue in performance, the use of different articulation for the two contrasting themes will assist in making the structure and architecture of the movement clearly audible throughout.

DOMINE DEUS

For the DOMINE DEUS, Bach writes a vocal duet. He represents the intimate relationship between the two persons of the Trinity who are called upon, God the Father and God the Son, by the simultaneous setting of the two texts *Domine Deus, Rex coelestis, Deus Pater omnipotens* ("O Lord God, King of heaven, God the Father Almighty") and *Domine Fili unigenite, Jesu Christe altissime* ("O Lord, Jesus Christ, the only-begotten Son, high above all") (ex. 39).

Ex. 39

Bach retains this compositional technique for the first half of the movement. In the second half, he purposely intensifies the expression by simultaneously giving both parts the same rhythm and text at *Domine Deus, Agnus Dei, Filius Patris* ("O Lord God, Lamb of God, Son of the Father") (ex. 40).

Ex. 40

The floating, suspended character of the instrumental setting is produced on one hand by the soloistic flute part, and on the other, by the string accompaniment, which Bach differentiates in an unusual manner by calling for the use of mutes on the violins while the bass instruments play pizzicato (ex. 41). The restrained setting for strings that results is

Ex. 41

extremely imaginative in its structure and surprisingly rich in its motivic variety. As early as the second bar, the rhythmically interesting writing in the second violin attracts notice. Then, in mm. 4-6, the first violin and continuo exchange a series of leaps of a sixth, introduced by an anacrusis of three sixteenths. Beginning in m. 7, the violins and violas proclaim a victorious motive consisting of three eighths, derived by inversion and rhythmic augmentation from the figuration being played simultaneously by the flute. Three expressive sighing motives of two slurred eighths follow in the strings in mm. 9 and 10. Then the violins and flute move upward together, the flute playing a "chain of sighs"—a rhythmic diminution of the previous string motive. Finally, the two-bar-long A^2 in the first violin (m.

13) defines the weightless character of the setting, before its resolution sets up the closing cadence (m. 16). This is an exceptionally elaborate accompaniment, considering that an accompaniment customarily stands in the background in favor of the solo instrument.

The multiplicity of motives and themes is also apparent in the two vocal parts. It is quite striking that Bach does not have the voices begin with the motives used by the instruments at the beginning of the movement; instead they begin with the expressive sighing symbol. The constant use of both voices together (except where one voice must rest to set up an imitative entrance) acquires a special significance in mm. 50-54 (ex. 42), where the common substance of God the Father and God the Son is symbolized by having both parts sing the same motive—the soprano in her low range, the tenor in his upper range. The expressive agitation of the following vocal fugato in which both parts begin high in the range and then fall (the tenor on *Deus Pater,* the alto on *Jesu Christe),* contrasts sharply with this symbol. This is emphasized by the sighing motives in the flute, and particularly, by the relative complex harmony in m. 53, where the scoring is reduced to three parts.

Ex. 42

In contrast with the motivic variety of the strings and voices, the flute concentrates primarily on a single expressive idea. Nearly all of the sixteenth-note figurations—the strings of sixteenths slurred by twos, as well as the arpeggios—flow into suspended notes, most of which are held for a quarter note before resolution. These suspended notes possess the expressive quality of the sighing motive; they pervade the entire setting and emphasize its sentiment.

It is likely that Bach chose to place such an imaginative movement at this point in the Mass in order to create a contrast with the preceding GRATIAS AGIMUS TIBI. The first three movements, ending with the objective, *stile-antico* setting of the GRATIAS AGIMUS TIBI, center on the praise of God. The differentiated variety of the DOMINE DEUS, however, begins a trio of pieces that are unified by the subjectivity of the prayer for God's mercy. In addition, it is noteworthy that a similar structural variety is to be observed in the CHRISTE ELEISON. The setting of the ET IN UNUM DOMINUM within the *SYMBOLUM NICENUM* features similar attributes as well. It appears that Bach deliberately endowed the Christ-centered duet movements with a variety of motives that accentuate their rhythmic activity and animation.

The duet is structured in four sections. Following the instrumental introduction and the associated vocal section, the introduction is taken up again in the middle of the piece (m. 60). The original is abridged by one modulatory measure (m. 63), but is repeated intact otherwise, now aiming toward a G-major cadence instead of the D-major of the introduction. The vocal segment that follows acquires its expressive intensification from the simultaneous use of the same text in both voices. But most importantly, the intensification stems from the modulation from the tonic key of G major and its related major keys, to the relative minor key of E minor. The textual appeal to the Lamb of God (*Agnus Dei*) foreshadows the immediately following QUI TOLLIS PECCATA MUNDI ("who takes away the sins of the world"), and the modulatory scheme aims toward the key of that movement. The tension in this section reaches its climax in m. 91, where Bach establishes the key of F-sharp major, which is emphasized by the sustained F-sharp in the flute. This key, the dominant of the B-minor tonality of the following movement, prepares the B-minor cadence that leads to the QUI TOLLIS PECCATA MUNDI.

The rhythmic treatment of the motives consisting of groups of two slurred sixteenth notes is of decisive significance in the shaping of the piece. Gerhard Herz[3] has established that the principal motive of the movement is notated in lombardic rhythm not only in the first measure of the autograph flute part, but also at later places in the autograph violin II and viola parts. This shows without a doubt that Bach intended this rhythm to be used in the principal motive, even where he did not explicitly notate it. The first bars in the flute and first violin should therefore be executed as follows (ex. 43).

Ex. 43

This rhythmic alteration should be used in all analogous places in the instrumental parts. Too, it should be used where groups of two slurred sixteenths appear, as in m. 4 of the flute part (ex. 44).

Ex. 44

This rhythm, which seems unusual at first glance, lightens even further the already weightless character of the movement established by the instrumentation. It follows logically that the sixteenth-note motion in the voice parts should be lombardic also.

Aside from the problems of lombardic rhythm, the major problem in the shaping of the movement is how to make audible the variety within the structure of the movement, despite its subdued restraint. In this regard it is important to provide subtle dynamic differentiation in the strings. The rhythmic component of the movement, emphasized by both the pizzicato of the continuo and the lombardic rhythm, should not obscure its basically relaxed, floating character. The continuo players must therefore deliberately play the pizzicato gently. In the second vocal section, on the words Agnus Dei, *the singers can achieve the essential building of intensity by a prudent building of dynamics. Most importantly, however, both vocalists must underscore the growing urgency of the movement by an expressively intense treatment of the text.*

QUI TOLLIS PECCATA MUNDI

Bach begins the choral movement QUI TOLLIS PECCATA MUNDI at the point where the principles of da-capo-aria composition dictate that the duet should return to the tonic key of G major. It is obvious from his autograph score that he intended a transition without pause: he did not place the usual fermata on the last chord of the solo section, nor did he use the customary double bar to show a transition between movements. The duet and the choral setting are to be understood as a single musical unit. The soloistically conceived appeals *Domine Deus, Agnus Dei, Filius Patris* ("Lord God, Lamb of God, Son of the Father") lead into the ensemble *miserere nobis* ("have mercy on us") and *suscipe deprecationem nostram* ("hear our prayers"). Instead of the flute Bach used previously, now he uses two; instead of a setting for two soloists, he uses a four-voice choir. This scoring establishes the restrained mood of the movement; the obbligato passages for the two flutes often move into a very low range, and the top voice is expressly assigned to the second soprano. The only other movement of the entire Mass in which the choir is deliberately reduced in size by the omission of the first soprano is the CRUCIFIXUS. (There are other movements with just four voice parts, but in these, the top part is explicitly designated for soprano I and II in unison.) Here we see clearly a characteristic Bach idea: that reflection upon the Lamb of God, who on the cross bore the sins of the world, is possible only in the tranquility of inward humility.

Bach acquired the QUI TOLLIS PECCATA MUNDI by reworking the opening chorus of Cantata BWV 46, *Schauet doch und sehet*, composed in 1723. The lament of Jerusalem, destroyed for its sins, *Schauet doch und sehet, ob irgend ein Schmerz sei, wie mein Schmerz, der mich troffen hat* (Lamentations 1:12: "Behold and see if there be any sorrow like unto my sorrow, which is done unto me."), which Bach deals with in the first movement of the cantata, is given new meaning as the fervent prayer for mercy to the Lamb of God, who takes away the sins of the world. The basic musical elements of both the cantata and Mass movements are identical (ex. 45). New to the Mass version of the

Ex. 45

movement, however, is the independent cello part within the continuo, which takes up with the explicitly marked *staccato* articulation the throbbing motive of the voice parts. This completes a most remarkable rhythmic structure within the instrumental setting. Four rhythms are layered upon each other: the quarter note followed by two quarter rests in the continuo, the continuous quarter notes in the cello, the eighth notes in the violins and violas, and the sixteenth-note motion in the flutes (ex. 46). Obviously, Bach wanted all elements of the orchestra to participate in the subjective expression of the movement, with increasing agitation from bottom to top.

Ex. 46

On one hand, the vocal setting obtains its special expressive strength from its harmonic content, which is characterized primarily by the leap of a sixth in the theme, the tension of dissonance on beat one of the measures following the long-held notes, and the subsequent chromatic resolution of the dissonance. On the other hand, it owes its strength to the variety within the theme, provided by the contrast between the repeated notes of the beginning and the melisma that immediately follows.

For the performance of the movement, it is crucial that the nearly static beginning of the theme and its quasi-expressive continuation be clearly articulated in each of the three fugato developments. However, the periods with the texts miserere nobis *("have mercy on us") and* deprecationem nostram *("our prayers") must stand in relief against the theme through the use of consistently legato articulation. The independent rhythmic motion of the continuo and cello must be clear enough so that when they abandon their independent lines from time to time in cadential measures (mm. 24-27, 38-41, and 48-50) and join into the expressive flow of the vocal setting, the change is clearly audible (ex. 47). The sixteenth-note movement in the flutes must always be heard against the underlying eighths in the strings. Above all, this is essential where groups of two slurred sixteenths urgently emphasize the words* miserere nobis *and* deprecationem nostram *in the closing bars of the individual sections.*

Ex. 47

QUI SEDES AD DEXTERAM PATRIS

The aria QUI SEDES AD DEXTERAM PATRIS is the third of the trio of "still" pieces that Bach placed at the core of his setting of the *GLORIA*. The restraint he intended is most clearly seen in his choice of solo instrument: though he employs regular oboes throughout the rest of the *GLORIA*, here he returns to the oboe d'amore. The movement acquires a mood of deliberate restraint from the choice of solo instrument and the fact that the string setting lacks obbligato function and serves merely as an accompaniment to the oboe.

Once again, Bach uses compositional technique symbolically. The close, canonic interweaving of the alto and the oboe and the immediately following unison writing for these solo parts (ex. 48)—a most unusual compositional device—once again relates to the different forms of being of the Father and the Son who sits at His right side, whose works meld together into one.

Ex. 48

Bach devotes special attention to the words *miserere nobis*, indicating "adagio" at a cadence-like point in the alto part (ex. 49) just a few bars after the repeat of the introduction in the dominant key. Twice in the instrumental setting of these measures (mm. 72-73) Bach

Ex. 49

writes a falling motive of two slurred eighth notes that is obviously directly related to the idea of the text (have mercy on us). This motive was previously an essential component of the fugue subject in the KYRIE ELEISON I (ex. 50). After concealed appearances in other

Ex. 50

movements, it appears conspicuously in the violins and violas of the DOMINE DEUS (ex. 51).

Ex. 51

In the QUI SEDES AD DEXTERAM PATRIS, it always occurs following the unison writing for the voice and oboe (mm. 22, 26, 47, and 72) (ex. 52); in the purely instrumental

Ex. 52

passages it occurs after the oboe and first violin play in unison (mm. 4, 16, 34, and 60). Bach employs this motive—which was shown to be of fundamental importance in the earlier discussion of the KYRIE ELEISON I—in deliberately conspicuous ways in the movements already mentioned, in order to deepen and intensify the suppliant expression of the plea for mercy. In the QUI SEDES AD DEXTERAM PATRIS, the motive, with its original "pianissimo" marking, almost acquires the expression of a physical gesture of supplication (like the publican in Luke 18:13, smiting his breast and pleading, "God, be merciful to me, a sinner"), in its proximity to the symbol-laden unison writing and the textual depiction of the majesty of God.

There are a number of possibilities for tempo in this aria. A very slow tempo, which would demand considerable sustaining power of the two soloists, would also provide the restraint that characterized the QUI TOLLIS PECCATA MUNDI, and thereby stress the gravity of the textual message. On the other hand, a faster tempo, in which the listener feels the half measure as the basic pulse, would release the meditative tension of the QUI TOLLIS PECCATA MUNDI and emphasize the playful component of the 6/8 meter. This faster tempo will also make the adagio measure discussed above stand out more clearly, in expressive emphasis of the words miserere nobis.

It is crucial to the shaping of the work that the performers differentiate clearly the various signs of articulation. The treatment of the staccato marks in the strings (ex. 53) is especially important. To Bach, these staccato marks signified only that the eighths were to

Ex. 53

be separated; they did not indicate the precise length of individual notes. A short articulation of these eighths, which perhaps would be quite charming in a suite movement, would
contradict the theme contained in the text and delineated by the structure of the aria. Thus,
the staccato-marked eighths must be definitely detached, but played relatively long.

QUONIAM TU SOLUS SANCTUS

What an extraordinary piece this is! Nowhere in Bach's entire cantata output does he
employ this scoring. The bass soloist is joined by three low obbligato instruments—a corno
da caccia and two bassoons—as well as the basso continuo. Bach's choice of such a unique
instrumentation is made all the more astonishing by the fact that two of the three obbligato
instruments—the corno da caccia and the second bassoon—appear nowhere else in the
GLORIA, not to mention the rest of the Mass. What was Bach's thinking in setting only this
portion of the text for bass and four low instruments, when the prominence of the words *tu
solus altissimus* ("You alone are high above all") suggests just the opposite?

The explanation is certainly that Bach wanted a contrast with the immediately following CUM SANCTO SPIRITU, the exuberant exultation of which appears to break out
from the low, restricted range of the QUONIAM TU SOLUS SANCTUS. Within this low
range of sound, Bach creates a very intense piece. The intensity of sound is produced
primarily by the scoring of the corno da caccia as the leading instrument: for this low-lying
movement, the horn has the same function as the first trumpet in the CUM SANCTO
SPIRITU that follows. Too, the main theme of the piece reinforces this intensity with the
determination of its octave leap and the fact that the intervallic content of the theme is
identical when read either forward or backward—symbolic of the perfection of the risen
Christ (ex. 54).

Ex. 54

41

In further contrast with the preceding aria, the other instruments are not merely accompanimental. Even the continuo frequently has a quasi-obbligato function; in m. 34, for example, it completes the main theme begun by the bass (ex. 55). The two bassoon parts

Ex. 55

are written in concertato fashion; they are characterized by a rhythmic variety to which Bach's articulatory signs give special prominence (ex. 56). They are also used to interpret

Ex. 56

the text, as when they ascend into their upper range on the words *Tu solus altissimus* (ex. 57).

Ex. 57

It is crucial for the shaping of this aria that the corno da caccia sound with intensity and strength. The continuo and the two bassoons, however, should never become merely a repressed, muttering background for the bass and horn. On the contrary, the entire movement must reflect the continuous activity that is created by the concertato writing of the individual parts. Though the QUONIAM TU SOLUS SANCTUS comes "out of the depths," it must still resound as an intense glorification of Christus altissimus—*"Christ, high above all."*

CUM SANCTO SPIRITU

The CUM SANCTO SPIRITU, which follows without pause the last chord of the QUONIAM TU SOLUS SANCTUS, is the brilliant conclusion of Bach's setting of the *Gloria* text. The performing forces—a choral-orchestral tutti—correspond to those of the first section of the *GLORIA*, but the CUM SANCTO SPIRITU surpasses the GLORIA IN EXCELSIS DEO in its concerted utilization of all the groups of the ensemble. Indeed, one would be hard pressed to find within Bach's works a more virtuosic piece for such a large scoring. The high notes of the fugue subject, the sixteenth-note runs of the countersubject, and the intricate rhythmic dovetailing of the counterpoint, place the greatest demands on the choir. In addition, Bach assigns concerted parts to the strings and woodwinds and gives the continuo (mm. 60-62) and the first trumpet (primarily from m. 122 to the end) tasks the difficulty of which far exceeds that of the earlier sections of the Mass.

In addition to this exceptionally virtuosic writing which Bach has deliberately withheld up to this time, he makes the structure of the movement serve the virtuosic nature of the piece. Several of the types of concertato composition that he used previously in the GLORIA IN EXCELSIS DEO appear again here, but the amazingly playful use of contrapuntal technique is new in the Mass: in the second of the two fugal expositions of the subject in the choir (the first with continuo only, the second with the orchestra), Bach surrounds each new entrance of the subject with entries of the other voices on the first few notes of the subject, only a quarter note apart (ex. 58). Here he is toying, so to speak, with the expectations of the listeners who are familiar with fugue: he leaves them wondering which of the various entries of the beginning of the subject will be extended into the complete subject.

Ex. 58

Bach structures the CUM SANCTO SPIRITU in five sections. In the first, third, and fifth sections, he sets the various groups of the ensemble (the choir, violins and violas, flutes and oboes, trumpets and timpani, and the independent continuo) against each other in concertato style. The different groups frequently exchange motives, and Bach brings them together in a deliberate crescendo through rising sequences that begin in the low range. The climax of the movement, which is also its vibrant conclusion, occurs following such an intensification (ex. 59, mm. 117-122), when the sixteenth-note motion of the first soprano—

Ex. 59

Fine

supported by the first violin and the woodwinds—passes to the first trumpet, which radiates above the entire movement with its high range and virtuosic rhythm (ex. 60, mm. 122-128).

For the second and fourth sections of the movement, Bach writes fugal expositions. The contrapuntal material for the fugue subject (ex. 60) has its origin in the motives of the

Ex. 60

concerted, tutti introduction. Rhythmically, the beginning of the subject is derived from the first four eighth notes of the voice parts at the beginning of the movement (ex. 61a). Intervallically, it comes from the frequent broken triads in the instrumental parts (ex. 61b).

Ex. 61

The group of four sixteenths in the subject was previously an obbligato figure in the instruments (ex. 62). In addition, the appearance of the threefold rising sequence in the

Ex. 62

subject was foreshadowed by another threefold sequence, though different in both rhythm and direction (ex. 63). Finally, even the sixteenth-note coloratura of the countersubject has

Ex. 63

its roots in the violin I part earlier in the movement (ex. 64).

Ex. 64

This intimate relationship between the concerted tutti sections and the fugal expositions that begin almost like chamber music, shows that even though Bach gave obvious prominence to virtuosic brilliance, he preserved the unity of the movement by the amazing logic of his treatment of the motivic and thematic materials.

The upward-moving sequences that start in the third measure of the subject and are sustained by the sixteenth-note motion of the countersubject (ex. 65), are evidence that the fugal sections are not intended to be purely motoric, despite their strongly rhythmic diction; they provide the music with a clearly linear component.

Ex. 65

It must always be the primary goal in the shaping of the work to project the concerted activity of the music while not permitting the previously discussed thematic and motivic work to become lost in a mass of undifferentiated sound. Bach's marking of "vivace" must be observed, but the lively tempo must not become hectic—this would detract from the otherwise often-playful character of certain portions of the movement, the fugues in particular. Clarity of texture must always be preserved, especially in those places where the various groups within the tutti are set against each other with different motivic materials. In the many places where the choir sustains chords through several bars (mm. 27-30, for example), it must hold back its sound to avoid hiding the obbligato parts in the orchestra. On the other hand, when the entire tutti has thematic material, it must possess real power and intensity. The articulation of the movement must be non-legato and staccato in order to project the concerto character of the music, but the instruction to play and sing "short" must not make the music appear trivial—the performers must always keep in mind its linear aspect, the constant forward drive to a climax. Finally, the function of this movement as the conclusion of Bach's KYRIE and GLORIA must be expressed in the deliberately emotional use of language by the choir, for here Bach brings together all of his vocal and instrumental forces, as well as all the possibilities of vocal and instrumental technique, in praise of the majesty of God. To quote Bach's own inscription under the last measure of his score: Fine—Soli Deo gloria ("The end. To God alone be the glory!").

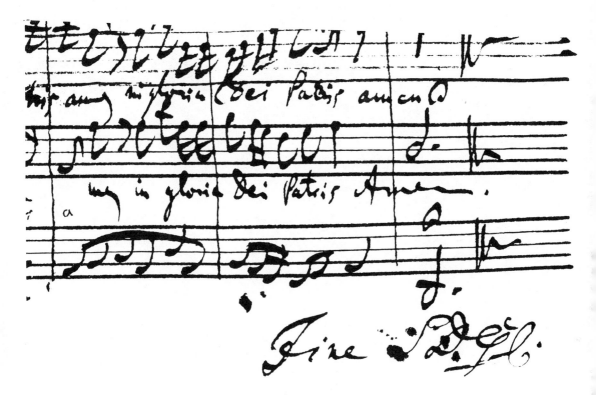

SYMBOLUM NICENUM (CREDO)

With the setting of the text of the *Credo*, the *Symbolum Nicenum* or Nicene Creed, we have before us the portion of the Mass that Bach did not conceive until his latter years. To be sure, in several places here, he makes use of some of his earlier works, just as he did in other sections of the Mass. But for the *CREDO,* the remodeling of previous compositions, a technique Bach used exclusively for the settings of the *OSANNA, BENEDICTUS, AGNUS DEI,* and *DONA NOBIS PACEM*, did not seem to satisfy him. He thus composed the CREDO IN UNUM DEUM, ET IN UNUM DOMINUM, ET INCARNATUS EST, ET IN SPIRITUM SANCTUM, and CONFITEOR UNUM BAPTISMA as completely new movements. Too, he modified the earlier pieces so thoroughly and placed them within the *CREDO* as a whole in such a way that they receive their full power of expression only in their context within the Mass text.

It is quite interesting to observe how Bach divided the text of the *Credo* into individual movements. (Asterisks denote newly composed pieces.)

*Movement 1:	CREDO IN UNUM DEUM,
Movement 2:	PATREM OMNIPOTENTEM, *factorem coeli et terrae, visibilium omnium et invisibilium.*
*Movement 3:	ET IN UNUM DOMINUM *Jesum Christum, Filium Dei unigenitum, et ex Patre natum ante omnia saecula. Deum de Deo, lumen de lumine, Deum verum de Deo vero. Genitum non factum, consubstantialem Patri, per quem omnia facta sunt. Qui propter nos homines et propter nostram salutem descendit de coelis.*
*Movement 4:	ET INCARNATUS EST *de Spiritu Sancto ex Maria Virgine et homo factus est.*
Movement 5:	CRUCIFIXUS *etiam pro nobis: sub Pontio Pilato passus et sepultus est.*
Movement 6:	ET RESURREXIT *tertia die, secundum scripturas. Et ascendit in coelum: sedet ad dexteram* [here Bach adds the word *Dei*] *Patris. Et iterum venturus est cum gloria judicare vivos et mortuos: cujus regni non erit finis.*
*Movement 7:	ET IN SPIRITUM SANCTUM, *Dominum et vivificantem, qui cum Patre et Filio simul adoratur et conglorificatur: qui locutus est per prophetas. Et unam sanctam catholicam et apostolicam ecclesiam.*
*Movement 8:	CONFITEOR UNUM BAPTISMA *in remissionem peccatorum et expecto resurrectionem mortuorum.*
Movement 9:	ET EXPECTO *resurrectionem mortuorum et vitam venturi saeculi. Amen.*

From this division of the text, it is clear that Bach intended from the outset to assign entire movements to the individual statements in the text that he believed the most significant, even if these often consisted of only a few words. Conversely, if the interpretation of specific statements in the text did not seem as important within the context of his setting of the *Credo* as a whole, he combined larger sections of text into a single movement. The forces Bach allots to each movement correspond to their relative importance, as shown already by his division of the text. The two longest, interrelated sections of text—*Et in unum Dominum* .... *descendit de coelis* and *Et in Spiritum Sanctum* .... *et apostolicam ecclesiam*—Bach gives to soloists; in contrast, he gives to the choir the shorter statements that were obviously more important to him.

In the layout of the movements, Bach follows the same procedure he did in earlier works such as the motet *Jesu meine Freude*, the *Magnificat*, the St. John Passion, and to a certain extent, the St. Matthew Passion: he uses a symmetrical framework that he constantly compresses toward the center of the work. The outer members of the structure consist of a pair of choral movements that are analogous in construction. At the beginning stands the quasi-a cappella CREDO IN UNUM DEUM and the orchestrally accompanied PATREM OMNIPOTENTEM. At the end Bach has the CONFITEOR UNUM BAPTISMA, which corresponds in compositional technique to the CREDO IN UNUM DEUM, followed by the ET EXPECTO, which is accompanied by the full orchestra. In the case of both pairs of movements, it was clearly Bach's conscious desire to join the a cappella movement intimately with the following tutti movement. This is shown by the fact that, in both cases, text from the first movement is taken up again at the beginning of the second.

Moving toward the center from these outer pairs of movements, we find two movements for soloists—first the ET IN UNUM DOMINUM (for soprano and alto), and then the ET IN SPIRITUM SANCTUM (for baritone). Thus, at the core of the *CREDO* stand three choral pieces that contain the three central ideas of Christological theology: the incarnation, the crucifixion, and the resurrection. This arrangement quite obviously places the CRUCIFIXUS at the center of the *CREDO* as a whole. Bach attached great significance to this trio of choral pieces, as shown by the fact that he had to rework his already completed setting of the ET IN UNUM DOMINUM duet, in which the words *Et incarnatus est de Spiritu Sancto ex Maria Virgine et homo factus est* appeared, in order to excise those words so that they might appear only in a choral movement devoted specifically to them. Bach's eagerness to have the CRUCIFIXUS at the center of his setting of the *CREDO* is shown by the fact that he undertook the troublesome revisions of the duet necessary to make the ET INCARNATUS EST into an independent choral movement which would, along with the choral ET RESURREXIT, provide a frame for the CRUCIFIXUS. Indeed, he was even willing to put up with the damage to the relationship between the text and the motives derived from it that resulted from his revision of the duet. (We will deal further with this idea in the discussion of the ET INCARNATUS EST, pp. 69-71.)

From the ideas presented above, the structure of Bach's setting of the *SYMBOLUM NICENUM*, with its focus on the CRUCIFIXUS, could be diagrammed as follows:

CREDO IN UNUM DEUM

PATREM OMNIPOTENTEM

ET IN UNUM DOMINUM

ET INCARNATUS EST

CRUCIFIXUS

ET RESURREXIT

ET IN SPIRITUM SANCTUM

CONFITEOR UNUM BAPTISMA

ET EXPECTO

CREDO IN UNUM DEUM

For this movement Bach writes a seven-part, motet-style setting, supported by continuo. Its theme is the Gregorian intonation to the *Credo* that was in use in the churches of Leipzig during Bach's time (ex. 66). The piece is written in the *stile antico*—the sixteenth-

Ex. 66

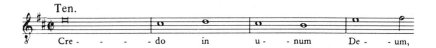

century style of church music typified by the works of composers such as Palestrina. Bach's choice of this style indicates his desire to avoid both a subjective interpretation of the text as well as concertato effects. Throughout nearly all of the piece, the two violin parts, which expand the five-part vocal setting into a seven-part, motet-style piece, are composed in a vocal style. With the exception of mm. 34 and 35, which we will discuss presently, and the final bars, in which the eighth-note motion foreshadows the following movement, they could easily have had text set to them (like many of the obbligato instrumental parts in works such as the *Psalmen Davids* of Heinrich Schütz).

The contrapuntal craft here is of the highest caliber. In the first exposition Bach presents the Gregorian theme in all parts but the continuo in the order tenor, bass, alto, soprano I, soprano II, violin I, and violin II. Then, in the second exposition, he omits the bass but otherwise retains the same order of entrances. Within this second exposition Bach compresses the structure: the two soprano entrances beginning in m. 21 are only one-and-one-half measures apart, and the same is true of the violin entrances beginning in m. 29. The movement reaches its climax with the third exposition of the theme, which begins in m. 33. Whereas Bach omitted the bass in the second exposition, here he brings it back with an augmentation of the theme. This is coupled with a duet in sixths on the original form of the theme in the second soprano and alto, the stretto-like imitation just a half note later in the first soprano, and the stretto duet in the two violins in m. 38. (ex. 67). Though the literal

Ex. 67

repetition of the first eight bars of the continuo in mm. 8-16 lends the movement a passacaglia-like character, the part is essentially thematically independent of the others. Even the continuous quarter-note motion in the continuo enters into the contrapuntal fabric: the writing for the first violin in mm. 34-35 (ex. 68a) bears a strong resemblance to the

Ex. 68a

opening bars of the continuo (ex. 68b). In addition, this portion of the violin part is actually a

Ex. 68b

retrograde diminution of mm. 7 and 8 of the continuo part.

By the avoidance of both concertato effects and subjective interpretation of the text in Bach's opening movement to his setting of the *Credo* text, he fuses himself with the history of the church and its music. On the other hand, he also understood the *Credo* as dogma, as "canon" in the Christian theological tradition, and he describes this dogma with all the techniques of canonic writing.

In the performance of this piece, the equal balance of the seven parts that join together in this motet-like structure is of great importance; the two obbligato violins must always be heard as clearly as the five choral parts. Since the second violin is difficult to hear in this dense texture, it could be reinforced by the addition of violas. The style of traditional vocal polyphony, which Bach employs here, demands a definite legato articulation to underscore the linear tension of the Gregorian theme. It is also essential that the theme be clearly defined rhythmically so that the contrapuntal work is clearly audible throughout. The performers can accomplish this through deliberately intensified choral diction and the use of accent in the violins. This is particularly important for the clarity of the stretto writing and the augmentation in the third exposition of the theme. The movement is really not in need of an interpretive dynamic scheme. The firmness and clarity of the compositional technique, unburdened by the need to interpret the meaning of the text, is consistent with a constant dynamic. This preserves the character of monumental objectivity, and climaxes occur as logical consequences of structural compression.

PATREM OMNIPOTENTEM

In each of the pairs of choral movements that open and close the *CREDO*, Bach used previously composed works as the basis for the second of the two movements. In the case of the PATREM OMNIPOTENTEM ("Father almighty"), he chose the opening movement of the 1729 cantata, *Gott, wie dein Name, so ist auch dein Ruhm* (BWV 171: According to Thy Name, O God, So Is Thy Glory). If one were to ask why Bach chose this particular cantata movement as the basis for his PATREM OMNIPOTENTEM, he would find the key to the understanding of the Mass movement in the text of the cantata movement, *Gott, wie dein Name, so ist auch dein Ruhm bis an der Welt Ende* ("According to Thy name, O God, so is Thy glory, even unto the ends of the earth"): it is not Bach's intention to *depict* the Creator, whose glory extends to the ends of the earth, but to *praise* Him.

Perhaps Bach had another reason for transplanting this specific cantata movement into the Mass. He was obviously concerned to write the *SYMBOLUM NICENUM* for five voices throughout, as witnessed by the fact that all of the newly composed choral movements are for five voices. In the ET EXPECTO Bach even took upon himself the trouble of adding a fifth voice to the four-voice cantata model. Only in the CRUCIFIXUS does he retain four voices—he expressly indicates that only the second soprano should sing the one soprano part, obviously underscoring the meditative restraint of this central movement. But why, then, did Bach not also rework the four-voice cantata movement, *Gott, wie dein Name*, for five voices, as he did with the ET EXPECTO—especially when the text seems to suggest an emphatic growth of intensity? The answer might well lie in the particular structure of the cantata movement. To be sure, the vocal setting is in four parts, but following the first exposition of the theme in the voices, Bach writes the theme as an obbligato part in the first trumpet, creating a five-part texture (ex. 69).

The text-related expression of these unusual techniques of composition and instrumentation is most clearly seen in the writing for the trumpet after the conclusion of the theme. The high, virtuosic eighth-note movement, which stretches the instrument to near its E^3 limit, gleams above the movement in symbolism of the glory of God, which extends "unto the ends of the earth" (ex. 69).

The closing bars provide one further example of the correspondence in meaning between the cantata and Mass movements. Here in the cantata Bach pictures the text *bis an der Welt Ende* (*visibilium omnium et invisibilium* in the Mass) with an ascending, scale-like figure that rises from a low D in the continuo to D^3 in the trumpet, filling the entire pitch spectrum with sound (ex. 70).

Despite these parallels, Bach changed his cantata model considerably in his new composition. The first such example is the fugue subject, the third bar of which is significantly altered on account of the new text (ex. 71). A later alteration of the soprano part is also

Ex. 71

Gott, wie dein Na - me, so   ist   auch dein Ruhm bis an der Welt En - de

Pa - trem o - mni - po - ten - tem, fa - cto - rem   coe - li et   ter - - rae,

interesting. At. m. 67 of the cantata movement, Bach writes the part in ex. 72. But at the

Ex. 72

bis   an   der   Welt En - - - - - - - de, der Welt   En - (de)

corresponding passage in the Mass, he writes as in ex. 73. The B natural in the soprano—

Ex. 73

et   in - vi - si - bi - li um vi - si - bi - li - um et   in - vi - si - bi - li - um

illogical in vocal writing and technically very difficult for the singer—is symbolic of the grasping at the barely tangible concept of invisibility.

But obviously, the objective of Bach's most critical alterations of the cantata model was to link the PATREM OMNIPOTENTEM as closely as possible to the CREDO IN UNUM DEUM. Whereas the cantata movement begins with the continuo-supported fugue subject alone, in the PATREM OMNIPOTENTEM Bach superimposes upon the beginning of the subject and four succeeding entries of it, a motive derived from the text of the preceding CREDO IN UNUM DEUM chorus (ex. 74). Bach used the key rela￼ ᵒnship

between the first two movements as yet another compositional device to tie them together. Even though the CREDO IN UNUM DEUM has only two sharps in the key signature—a reflection of the fact that the modal cantus firmus is transposed up a whole tone—the movement begins and ends in A major. Had Bach kept the cantata model intact, he would have begun the PATREM OMNIPOTENTEM in clear D major, which would have emphasized the division between the two movements. This is precisely what he wished to avoid. He added six new measures to the beginning of the cantata movement and began with an A-major statement of the subject in the bass. Though the tonality is obscured by the G natural in the second bar of the continuo, it is immediately confirmed by the G sharps in the bass and continuo in m. 4. In addition, Bach buries the tenor entrance in m. 7 so deeply in the texture that the tonic key of the second movement—D major—is not stabilized until m. 12. One could even go as far as to say that the unequivocal establishment of D major requires the pedal point in m. 65 and the dominant-tonic entrance of the timpani in m. 67.

Finally, one cannot help but notice the strong connection between the continuo parts of both movements. The quarter notes at the beginning of the CREDO IN UNUM DEUM constitute a nearly exact inversion in augmentation of the eighth notes in the continuo at the beginning of the PATREM OMNIPOTENTEM. The ascending, diatonic sequences of four quarter notes at a time in the first movement, as for example in m. 4, have a parallel in the groups of four diatonically ascending eighths that appear for the first time in m. 4 of the PATREM OMNIPOTENTEM (ex. 75a&b).

Ex. 75a

CREDO IN UNUM DEUM:

Ex. 75b

PATREM OMNIPOTENTEM:

Why did Bach want to tie the two opening movements together in so many ways? An explanation must start with the fact that Bach was entirely conscious of the inseparability of the components of the sentence *Credo in unum Deum, Patrem omnipotentem, factorem coeli et terrae, visibilium omnium et invisibilium.* Since, despite the unity of this text, he attempted to set it in two different forms and styles, and to connect the two resulting movements as intimately as possible, it seems that he wished to present the CREDO IN UNUM DEUM as dogma, free of any subjective elements. When the text is accepted as reality in the PATREM OMNIPOTENTEM, it turns into a glorification of God that extends "unto the ends of the earth."

In the shaping of the work for performance, the use of the same basic tempo in both of the introductory movements is the clearest way to show the unity for which Bach so obviously strove. Since the basic rhythmic pulse in the CREDO IN UNUM DEUM is the half note, as opposed to the quarter note in the PATREM OMNIPOTENTEM, the tempo appears to double going from the first movement to the second, even though the half note remains constant. While this tempo relationship underlines the unity of the movements, it is also appropriate to the differing styles of the two pieces—the motet style of the first as opposed to the concerto style of the second. There should be no pause between the two movements. The most natural solution to the problem of transition is the use of the end of the final chord of the CREDO IN UNUM DEUM as the anacrusis to the beginning of the PATREM OMNIPOTENTEM.

The major interpretive problem in the shaping of the PATREM OMNIPOTENTEM is the clarification of the concertato activity of the movement. To this end, rhythmic precision and vitality as well as dynamic intensity are important. The impact of the climaxes marked by the entrances and part writing of the trumpets can be reinforced by having the trumpets relax their intensity in those measures in which there is no working over of the thematic material.

ET IN UNUM DOMINUM

Bach begins his setting of the second article of faith, which speaks of belief in Jesus Christ, the Son of God, with a duet. Just as in the CHRISTE ELEISON, this use of two voices is meant to symbolize the second person of the Trinity. The text contains many references to the consubstantiality of the Father and the Son who "proceeds from Him," as well as the differences between these two personages of God: *Et ex Patre natum, Deum de Deo, lumen de lumine, Deum verum de Deo vero, genitum non factum,* and *consubstantialem Patri* ("born of the Father," "God of God," "light of light," "true God of true God," "begotten, not made," and "of one substance with the Father"). Bach expresses this simultaneous unity and difference between the Father and the Son in a single motive, which appears canonically in m. 1 in the two highest orchestral parts and continues to pervade the entire movement (ex. 76). The notes of the motive are identical in both parts, a representa-

Ex. 76

tion of the common substance of the Father and the Son. But the articulation is different, the last two eighths in the first part being marked staccato, while the same notes in the second part are slurred. The first motive, the stronger of the two, represents the all-powerful Father; the second motive, a gentler musical gesture, represents the Son, who proceeds from the Father. This perfect musical synonym for the meaning of the text permeates the entire movement.

Two versions of the duet exist. In the first version (NBA edition, pp. 148-156), Bach included the text of the second article of faith from its beginning (*Et in unum Dominum*), through *Et incarnatus est*, to *et homo factus est*. It is quite obvious that some of the individual passages of the text inspired specific musical ideas within the movement. The descending figure that occurs for the first time in mm. 59 and 60, falling from the first violin through the entire string section, is a visual and aural painting of the descent from heaven of the Son of God (ex. 77). After the domination of the entire movement by G major and its

Ex. 77

related keys, the startling change to E-flat major in m. 69 is explainable only by the text *et homo factus est* ("and was made man"), which appears here for the first time: God totally transforms the nature of His being and enters into an entirely different kind of world. Furthermore, this is the only place in the movement where Bach abandons the otherwise simultaneous use of the two forms of the primary motive that differ only in their articulation. In this section, only the slurred motive associated with Christ appears (ex. 78, intact in m. 70 and varied in m. 71)—perhaps as an intentional emphasis of the text *et homo factus est?*

Ex. 78

Measure 63 and the following measures provide another interesting insight into Bach's way of working. To be analogous with the movement up to this point, a ritornello would have to follow again here, dividing the present text from the one before. With the return to the tonic key of G major in m. 63, we have at the same time a return to the beginning—the da capo of the movement. To be sure, Bach begins this da capo with the instruments alone in the first bar, but then he adds the voices in the second and third bars, on the words *et incarnatus est*. Thus, the soprano and alto are not merely superimposed upon the instrumental setting, but rather, they are at its core, symbolic of Christ's birth into the midst of the world. To this end, in the upper two parts in m. 66 (violin 1 and oboe 1, violin 2 and oboe 2), Bach uses a motive that he quite obviously wanted to associate with the words *et incarnatus est*; it attracts attention because of its unusual slurred-staccato articulation (ex. 79). The

motive appears for the first time in mm. 21 and 22, on the text *et ex Patre natum* ("and was born of the Father") (ex. 80); here it is thus a musical synonym for the life-giving descent of the Spirit of God.

Ex. 80

It has already been shown that the reason for Bach's decision to compose a new, choral setting of the ET INCARNATUS EST lay in considerations of the form of the *CREDO* as a whole—within the framework of his setting of the *CREDO*, the CRUCIFIXUS was to be the central movement. But why did Bach not leave the duet just as it was, rather than undertake a revision in which he abbreviated the text so that the piece extended only through the words *descendit de coelis*? In the revision, Bach left the instrumental setting intact, but he had to recompose the voice parts, in the process degrading the close text-music relationship that characterized the original version. It must certainly have been Bach's desire in his final version of the *CREDO* not just to put the CRUCIFIXUS at the center, but also to give the setting of the text *et incarnatus est* an importance equal to the ET RESURREXIT. On one hand, he accomplishes this by the composition of the choral movement to the *et incarnatus* text; on the other hand, it seems that it was unthinkable to him to treat the text to which he had given so much emphasis in the choral movement, in a less important way in the preceding duet. Quite the contrary, it appears that it was important to him to create a clear division between the choral setting and the duet, since he begins the ET INCARNATUS EST with a three-measure instrumental introduction.

Thus, in no way is the textually abbreviated version of the ET IN UNUM DOMINUM duet a "variant," as it is called in the *Neue Bach Ausgabe*; rather, it is Bach's final, definitive version of the movement and it must not be replaced arbitrarily by the earlier version. The use of the original form of the duet can be justified only if the choral ET INCARNATUS EST is omitted at the same time, restoring the *CREDO* as a whole to its earlier form.

It is of the utmost importance in the musical shaping of the movement that there be a distinct difference between the two forms of the principal motive. The first, staccato-marked form must not just be played "short." As the musical image of the first person of the Trinity, God the Creator, it must have a rather vigorous, marcato character. The dialogue character that dominates the entire movement must always be perceptible. Although the ritornellos have an ensemble character and therefore require a natural intensity, the alternating dialogue between sustained notes and figurations in the two upper instrumental parts must always remain clear. The dialogue between the two solo voices begins each of the individual sections of the movement with a quiet restraint brought about by the low tessitura. The tension that develops from the restraint of these sectional beginnings must have its climax in m. 56, where both voices come together rhythmically for the first time, and the viola, which had hardly any thematic material before, assumes an expressive, obbligato function. Following this intensification, the last section of the movement must begin with the greatest restraint. The accompanying orchestra must never force the low-lying voice parts to sing loudly. Likewise, it would be natural for the unusually low conclusion of the voice parts that follow the strong E-flat-major bars (mm. 70-72) to be matched by a piano dynamic in the orchestral measures that follow.

ET INCARANTUS EST

The choral setting of the text *Et incarnatus est de Spiritu Sancto ex Maria Virgine et homo factus est* that Bach composed for his final version of the *CREDO* is characterized by multiple references to the sign of the cross.

The visual symbol of the cross is to be found in the violin motive that pervades the movement. If the second note is connected to the fifth and the third is connected to the fourth, the result is a reclining cross, which is also the Greek letter *chi*, the initial letter of the word *Christos* (ex. 81). The descending fugato motive in all five choral parts on the words *Et*

Ex. 81

incarnatus est is clearly related to the music to which the words *descendit de coelis* were set in the original version of the preceding duet, ET IN UNUM DOMINUM. (See ex. 78), mm. 59-61.) Each of the two sections in which the fugato motive is developed is composed in such a way that the fourth note of the bass, the last part to enter, is sharped (ex. 82). This sharp,

Ex. 82

which is also a form of cross (the German words for "sharp" and "cross" are identical), marks the end of the series of motives that represent the incarnation of Christ. In both development sections, this chromaticism in the bass ends the pedal point and begins the harmonic motion of the movement.

Despite the cross symbolism, both developments of the text *Et incarnatus est de Spiritu Sancto ex Maria Virgine et homo factus est* are characterized more by a meditative, almost mystical restraint, than by a direct connection with the following CRUCIFIXUS. This changes, however, with the words *et homo factus est* in the final section of the piece. In the chromatic alto part in mm. 41-44, Bach quotes the passacaglia theme of the following movement in retrograde, altered rhythmically and transposed up a fifth. In the following measures, he intensifies the idea of the cross by writing in the continuo, violin II, and violin I, three canonic imitations of the motive that had previously been in unison in the violins, with each entrance only a quarter note apart (ex. 83).

Ex. 83

These two techniques—the statement of the coming chromatic passacaglia theme in the alto and the canonic compression of the cross motive—produce a rather abrupt compression of the movement and thereby, the transition to the CRUCIFIXUS.

In the performance of the movement, the numerous musical symbols must not entice one to ignore its structure. Not until the CRUCIFIXUS does Bach reduce the choir to four parts; here in the ET INCARNATUS he still writes for five voices and takes the individual parts into such high tessituras that a real pianissimo would be an unnatural, artificial-sounding effect. The three sections of the movement should begin with restraint, as suggested by the modest scoring and the static repetition of the notes in the continuo (which is related to the continuo parts of the QUI TOLLIS PECCATA MUNDI and the CRUCI-FIXUS). But in the first and second sections, the upward motion of all parts on the words ex

70

Maria Virgine produces distinct intensifications of sound that have their climaxes in the closing, cadential bars. The compositional compression that occurs in mm. 40-48, on the words et homo factus est *(the quotation of the previous fugato motive in the second soprano, the upward motion of the other voices, the allusion to the passacaglia theme of the CRUCIFIXUS in the alto, and finally, the canonic writing in the upper three voice parts and most importantly, in the three instrumental parts) must be reflected in an immediate, almost passionate growth of intensity and volume that will dissipate the mystical rapture of the beginning of the movement and simultaneously foreshadow the immediately following CRUCIFIXUS.*

CRUCIFIXUS

The CRUCIFIXUS is the center of Bach's setting of the *CREDO*. Surrounded by movements that correspond to each other in symmetrical structure, the CRUCIFIXUS treats the text that appears to have been the most important to Bach: *Crucifixus etiam pro nobis sub Pontio Pilato, passus et sepultus est.* The musical setting of this movement is an adaptation of the opening choral movement to the 1714 cantata *Weinen, Klagen, Sorgen, Zagen,* BWV 12. The fact that Bach would fall back upon the music of an earlier work for his setting of this crucial text shows once again that he did not consider the reworking of a pre-existant piece to be an inferior method of composition. In comparison with the other parody movements in the Mass, Bach made relatively minor revisions to the portion of the cantata model he used in his construction of the musical setting of the CRUCIFIXUS. He transposed the prototype from F minor to E minor and reduced the five-part, divided-viola string texture typical of the early cantatas to the usual, four-part string texture. In addition, in those places where the string parts of the cantata movement have rests on the second beat of the measure, he used the flutes to provide a complementary rhythm. Even with these changes, the resulting passacaglia-based orchestral setting remains in the background relative to the vocal parts, just as it had in the cantata.

The passacaglia theme is not of Bach's invention. Rather, it is the so-called *lamento bass,* a bass line widely used in the seventeenth and eighteenth centuries, especially in chaconne-type compositions. In the cantata Bach wrote it in half notes, but for the Mass, he breaks it into quarters (ex. 84a), creating a rhythmically intensified foundation for the

Ex. 84a

movement, which is characterized otherwise by motion in half and whole notes. The continous, repeated-note motion in quarters also produces a pulsing or throbbing—an expression he intended to be analogous to that created by the continuo line of the QUI TOLLIS (ex. 84b).

Ex. 84b

A whole series of smaller alterations demonstrates the pains Bach took to modify the music he had composed for the relatively general text of the cantata ("Tears, laments, sorrows, fears, anxiety, and need are the bread of the Christian's tears.")—to suit the specific interpretation of the Mass text ("He was crucified also for us: under Pontius Pilate He suffered and was buried"). The most striking alteration occurs in mm. 9 and 10 of the cantata (mm. 13 and 14 of the Mass), where he rewrites the soprano and alto parts to sharpen the expression of the word *crucifixus* (ex. 85).

Ex. 85

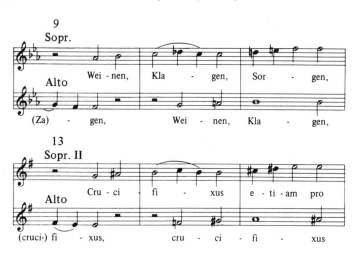

If one considers the vocal setting as a whole, it is apparent that, even before Bach's modifications, the cantata movement contained a continual compression and intensification of structure that reaches its climax at the beginning of variation 10. (See example 87, which contains the complete vocal setting of the CRUCIFIXUS.) After an introductory, purely instrumental variation, Bach makes interpretive use of this compression to give special attention to specific portions of the Mass text; up to m. 37, he consistently combines two of the four-measure variations for the treatment of a single textual statement. This technique allowed Bach to give a very different expression to each segment of the text. In mm. 5-12, the focus is solely on the word *crucifixus*, which, sung twice by each of the four voices, establishes the character of restrained lament of the opening meditation. In the fourth and fifth variations (mm. 13-20), no longer do the individual voices trail off aimlessly and haltingly; instead, they move to linear climaxes. In addition, one can see specific musical interpretations of the text, such as the soprano part on the final *pro nobis* (mm. 15-16) or the sustained tenor in mm. 17-18: the held syllable of the word *crucifixus* (*-fix-*) being the Latin stem for "to sustain." Variations 6 and 7 (mm. 21-28) witness further structural compression, brought about by the imitation of the chromatic motives related to the passacaglia theme. The most important manifestation of this is the stretto on the passacaglia theme between the continuo and the tenor in mm. 23-26. No longer does the word *crucifixus* appear; instead the attention turns to the three words *etiam pro nobis*, and of these, particularly to *etiam*, on which the imitation begins. For further structural compression, in variations 8 and 9 (mm. 29-36), Bach continues the simultaneous, homophonic use of all four voices, a texture already established at the end of the previous variation. These variations contain two developments of the text *passus et sepultus est*. Noteworthy in the first variation is the downward voiceleading which corresponds to the meaning of the text. This is counteracted in the next variation by the upward motion of the voices and the rhythmic intensification. In variations 10, 11 and 12 (mm. 37-48), Bach repeats the entire text. This repetition of a lengthy, already through-composed section of text is unique in the Mass. In this central movement of the *CREDO*, it seems as if Bach wished to intensify this central statement, which had already been reflected upon in the preceding variations. This applies especially to the setting of the word *crucifixus* in the tenth variation: the vocal parts here are among the most dissonant Bach ever composed. Having already seen the symbol of the cross in the ET INCARNATUS EST, one would certainly expect to find it in Bach's *CRUCIFIXUS*: it appears now in the soprano in mm. 37-39.

In the twelfth variation, the setting of the text *sepultus est* ("and was buried"), Bach modifies the music of the cantata model in order to depict the new text: the alto and tenor now move into their low ranges, and the bass cadences on a low E that has not been heard heretofore. It would be perfectly possible for the CRUCIFIXUS to conclude here, but the next movement, the ET RESURREXIT, must begin in D major because of the D trumpets. Since in the harmonic language of Bach's time, D major could not directly follow E minor, Bach modulates to the subdominant of D major, G major. Bach's completion of this modulation in variation 13, from mm. 49-53, is admirable. First, he adopts the idea of the preceding variation, and a musical synonym for the word *sepultus*, writes in ever-lower tessituras until the closing G-major chord. In addition, in the course of the modulation, he is able gradually to reduce the cruelty and harshness of the text *passus et sepultus est*, so that the splendor of the coming ET RESSUREXIT seems to be superimposed upon the end of the CRUCIFIXUS (ex. 86).

Ex. 86

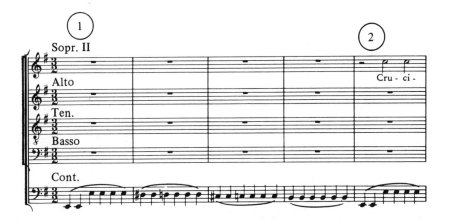

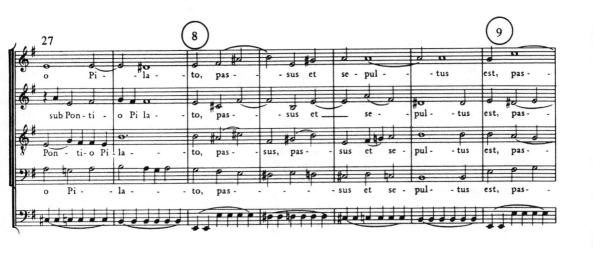

Having examined this movement in such detail, it is interesting to pose once again a basic question: why did Bach compose the CRUCIFIXUS in the form of a passacaglia? This question is of particular importance, since all of the other forms he uses in the course of the Mass (fugue, da-capo aria, quasi-motet, concerto, etc.) appear several times, but the CRUCIFIXUS is the sole movement set as a passacaglia. The employment of this form—a series of variations over a constant, repeating bass theme—at the place Bach so deliberately planned as the center of the *SYMBOLUM NICENUM*, shows that he interpreted the text as an article of faith too important to mention only once. Rather, it is the constantly recurring, central tenet of the Christian faith.

The musical shaping of the movement is prescribed in large part by the ideas presented above. As a consequence of Bach's reduction of the choir to four voices—he expressly indicates "soprano II"—there spans an arch of constant intensification from the thin texture and resulting restraint of variations 2 and 3 to the climax of the dissonant variation 10. The relaxation of sound begins at the end of the eleventh variation and continues in a constant diminuendo through the ever-lower-moving setting, until the end of the final chord. The spectrum of expression that is available for the interpretation of the text ranges from the plaintive restraint of the beginning, where one hardly dares utter the word crucifixus, *to the piercing sharpness and uncompromising harshness that characterize the dissonant entrances in the tenth variation. The choir can project these gradations of expression through deliberate variations in the character of its diction.*

One might approach the flow of tension in the movement in a number of different ways. On one hand, it would be possible to vigorously reinforce the compression of structure with a growth of intensity through variation ten and a subsequent relaxation to the end. Alternatively, considering the location of the movement in the SYMBOLUM NICENUM *and the explicit omission of the first soprano, one could perform it with restrained dynamics throughout, in order to provide a sharp contrast with the following ET RESURREXIT. Of course, many intermediate solutions are possible, depending on the perceptions of the conductor and the spirit of the moment of performance. In any case, the passacaglia theme, with its omnipresent throbbing, must remain audible throughout.*

76

ET RESURREXIT

All of the previous movements of the SYMBOLUM NICENUM have been characterized by the use of a vocally-oriented compositional technique. Both the textual-declamation-derived themes and Bach's development of them were taken up by the instruments as well as the voices. When there were independent instrumental themes, as for example, in the ET INCARNATUS EST and the ET IN UNUM DOMINUM, they did not represent the primary substance of the movement. The reve se is true in the ET RESURREXIT. The piece is in the form of a concerto movement, the instrumentally conceived themes of which tend toward the virtuosic. In several ways, the music exhibits the typical characteristics of Bach's concerto movements as well as a surprising resemblance to the opening movement of the *Third Brandenburg Concerto* and similar instrumental works: the trill-like sixteenth-note figuration (as in the soprano I in mm. 28-31) (ex. 87), the

Ex. 87

constant alternation of sixteenths with triplets of sixteenths (for example, in the flutes, ex. 88), and the clearly recognizable concerto technique of writing for individual instrumental

Ex. 88

groups as well as their fusion in a tutti texture. It thus seems reasonable to speculate that Bach used a now-lost concerto movement as the basis for the ET RESURREXIT.

For the first time in the *SYMBOLUM NICENUM*, Bach employs the full orchestra, including the flutes. In further contrast with the preceding movements, he repeatedly writes longer sections for the instruments alone. From the four-voice scoring of the preceding CRUCIFIXUS, he now returns to a five-voice chorus and writes for it in the same virtuosic concerto style as the instruments. Thus, all the instrumental and vocal forces combine within a virtuosic concerto movement to depict vitally and enthusiastically the jubilation of the resurrection of Christ.

Bach's desire to have a sharp, even blatant contrast between the CRUCIFIXUS and the ET RESURREXIT is shown by the nature of the "seam" between the two movements. Following the composed diminuendo in the final bars of the CRUCIFIXUS, in which only the voices and continuo are used and descend to their deepest ranges, the ET RESURREXIT begins with the most massive orchestration and in a high range—the tenors of a high A^1. Nowhere in the history of Mass composition is the belief in the resurrection expressed with such absolute confidence as it is here.

The main theme of the movement (ex. 89)—with its fanfare beginning and symmetrical construction (the pitches read identically both forward and backward)—is powerful, but

Ex. 89

general enough in character that it can be used with such different textual ideas as *et resurrexit, et ascendit in coelum, et iterum venturus est,* and *cujus regni non erit finis.* Despite this unifying thematic connection, Bach is able to interpret differently each of these segments of text. Within the first section, in which Bach sets the text *Et resurrexit tertia die secundum scripturas* ("And the third day He rose again, according to the scriptures,"), one finds a fugato characterized by running sixteenths (ex. 90), which is developed from a motive

Ex. 90

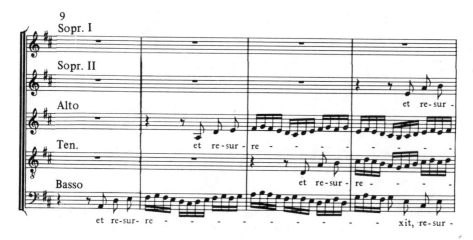

derived from the main theme. It is tempting to interpret this as an image from the Easter story, in which the news of Christ's resurrection spreads like wildfire from one person to another. Then in m. 14, again on the words *et resurrexit*, the choir and orchestra come together homophonically, triumphantly surpassing the intensity of the beginning of the movement with the ascent of the first soprano to a high B^2.

After the text-related ascending scale in the first soprano in m. 19 (ex. 91), doubled by

Ex. 91

re - sur - re - xit ter-ti - a   di - e,

the first violin and first oboe, mm. 28-32 are of particular interest (ex. 92). The sixteenth-

note motive of the previously mentioned fugato is now modified and taken up again with greater urgency. The violins and violas, as well as the alto, tenor, and bass, constantly move upward from the low register with fanfare-like arpeggios. The most striking of all the musical elements here is the chromatically ascending continuo line. The antithetical meanings of the texts *Crucifixus....passus et sepultus est* and *Et resurrexit* have their motivic analogy here in the use of a chromatically ascending continuo line that approximates an inversion of the passacaglia theme. The later settings of statements related in meaning to *et resurrexit—et ascendit in coelum* ("and He ascended into heaven") and *cujus regni non erit finis* ("of His kingdom there shall be no end")—contain the same symbolic motive in the continuo. Although the inversion is not complete, Bach's intention to provide an analogy to the CRUCIFIXUS theme is further evidenced by his use of a similar rhythm and articulation, i.e., repeated notes, slurred by sixes.

The next vocal section is a setting of the text *et ascendit in coelum; sedet ad dexteram Dei Patris* ("And He ascended into heaven: He sits at the right hand of God the Father"). Here we have a whole series of ways of writing for the voices, all of which depict the word *ascendit*. In mm. 50 and 51, where the new text appears for the first time, the tenor leaps up a fifth with a vigorous, syncopated counterrhythm (ex. 93). In m. 58 both the tenor and the

Ex. 93

second soprano enter into the orchestral passage with octave leaps upward (ex. 94). In

Ex. 94

addition, one is struck by the musical figures that depict with vital intensity the ascension of Christ: the upward arpeggios in the violins and violas in mm. 60 and 62; the similar writing for the choir (especially the bass) in m. 61; and the continuo, which once again builds upward chromatically. The focal point of both this modulation and the meaning of the text is in m. 63. Here Bach describes the steadfast majesty of Christ by the octave leap down on the word *sedet* ("sits")—a contrast with the preceding ascending lines—and the syncopated motive that appears a quarter note apart in the other voices (ex. 95).

Ex. 95

The third section of the movement, the setting of the text *et iterum venturus est cum gloria judicare vivos et mortuos* ("And He shall come again with glory to judge both the living and the dead"), differs in character from the other sections in that it is dominated by minor keys—first B minor, the relative minor of the tonic D major; then F-sharp minor, the relative minor of the dominant. The specific message of the text here makes itself known in the ritornello even before the choir enters, when the sustained trill-like sixteenth-note motion previously confined to the upper parts of the choir and orchestra (m. 16, for example), is shifted to the orchestral bass part in mm. 68 and 70. This continuo writing, which Bach brings to the fore through the rests in the violins and violas and the merely accompanimental eighths in the woodwinds, rather abruptly intensifies the instrumental setting and restlessly, even threateningly, sets the stage for the return of Christ and the Last Judgement, the subjects of the following measures (ex. 96).

Ex. 96

The following vocal section (ex. 97) brings with it a decrease in the scoring to a mere two parts; besides the bass, only the continuo has an obbligato function, and the eighth notes in the violins and violas serve only to clarify the chords in the continuo. It is obvious that Bach deliberately dispenses with the brilliance of the concertato orchestra here and transfers the activity to the two lowest parts of the setting. Here one is reminded of the account of the "great day of His wrath" in Revelation, when the sun "becomes black as sackcloth," the full moon "becomes like blood," and the stars crash to earth (Revelation 6:12 ff.). It is in such a darkened setting that Bach depicts with extreme intensity the second coming of Christ and His judgement. This manifests itself first in the variety of rhythms of the vocal bass, the first measures of which are still loosely patterned on the main theme of the movement. But then, on the words *judicare vivos et mortuos*, Bach deliberately avoids the use of rhythmic sequence and destroys the sense of downbeat accent by the use of counter accents. The Day of Judgement is depicted with great agitation and forcefulness by the furious vehemence of the constant upbeat runs in both the voice and continuo, the frequent crossings of these parts, and the exploitation of the entire range of the bass voice—with the symbolically high tessitura for *vivos* and the very low setting of *mortuos* in mm. 85 and 86. This choral passage of such great technical difficulty for just a single voice part is unique in Bach's vocal works. For this reason, as well as the fact that similar two-part passages (voice and continuo) in Bach's music are almost invariably for soloists, it might seem desirable for a soloist to perform this passage. But this would suit neither Bach's depiction of the text, which has its own forceful impetus, nor the universal nature of the words, which is expressed through the use of the choir.

Bach uses da-capo technique for the composition of the fourth section of text, *cujus regni non erit finis* ("of His kingdom there shall be no end"). The beginning of the da capo is an almost literal repetition. Aside from a total of eight measures that are omitted here (mm. 7 and 8 and mm. 14-19 in the first section of the movement), the periodic construction of related measures and the motivic treatment are essentially identical. The tutti entrance on the first *cujus regni* receives its great expressive strength from the intentional contrast with the immediately preceding F-sharp-minor chord with its low bass F sharp, just as the beginning of the movement was set apart by the contrast with the preceding, low-lying *sepultus est*. The terror of the Last Judgement is dissipated by the assurance of God's eternal dominion. Despite the close affinity with the first section of the movement, here Bach succeeds in making the music suit his new text by bringing in the trumpets and timpani more often than before. The first such appearance is in mm. 93 and 94, where the high trumpet parts provide a bright intensification of the chords at the beginning of the choral fugato (ex. 98). Then, from m. 101, Bach unequivocally hands the lead to the trumpets,

Ex. 98

whereas at the parallel spot in the opening section (m. 24), the chorus had the lead instead of the flutes, which played *colla parte*. To be sure, the soprano I and alto are doubled here as well by the trumpets. But it is quite obvious that Bach intended the trumpets, particularly the first, to dominate: he writes the first-trumpet part an octave higher than the alto (ex. 99).

The intensified use of the trumpets for the last section of the movement should not be understood merely as a general building of sound. The importance of this event lies much more in the fact that to Bach, the trumpet was the "regal" instrument, which he brought in many times in his cantatas when the subject turned to God the King. Thus, the reason for the almost-constant trumpet accompaniment in this final section of the movement lies in the text, which speaks of the reign of God. This is most clearly seen at the end of the vocal section, where Bach frees the first trumpet from the accompanying instruments and the first soprano, takes it up to D^2 with vital rhythm, and thereby crowns the setting of the text *cujus regni non erit finis* with a triumphant conclusion (ex. 100).

The performance of the entire movement must exude concertato vitality. This requires a tempo fast enough to make the virtuosic component of the movement immediately perceptible. For example, musical events such as the trill-like sixteenth-note figuration in the first soprano in mm. 28-31 and the two trumpet parts in the closing orchestral section must have an unequivocal, forward-pressing character. On the other hand, the tempo must be slow enough to guarantee a flawless choral performance of the technically exacting *sixteenth-note triplets. Too, the intensity-oriented dynamic shaping of the movement is in need of strong differentiation, if aspects of the compositional structure are not to be lost. For example, the intensification of the portions of the movement built upon the chromatic continuo line (mm. 28-32, 60-63, 105-109, and 125-129) is possible only if there is careful relaxation during the preceding bars. Too, it is very important to the clarity of texture of the movement that certain groups within the ensemble recede into the background so that others might lead. This is especially true in the instrumental sections, where the alternation of wind soloists with the orchestral tutti is clearly seen in the compositional structure.*

ET IN SPIRITUM SANCTUM

In the introductory remarks on the overall form of Bach's setting of the *SYMBOLUM NICENUM*, it was observed that he allotted entire movements to those statements he considered the most important, even though they might consist of just a few words. In contrast with this, in the ET IN SPIRITUM SANCTUM aria, he sets the longest internally coherent passage of text in the entire *CREDO*. It consists of a whole series of statements that require musical interpretation: *Et in Spiritum Sanctum, Dominum et vivificantem, qui ex Patre Filioque procedit, qui cum Patre et Filio simul adoratur et conglorificatur: qui locutus est prophetas. Et unam sanctam catholicam et apostolicam ecclesiam.* ("And [I believe] in the Holy Spirit, the Lord and giver of life, who proceeds from the Father and the Son, who together with the Father and the Son is worshipped and glorified: who spoke by the prophets. And in one holy catholic and apostolic church.") The sheer volume of text to be packed into a single movement is itself an indication that, in the interest of the overall view of the setting of the *SYMBOLUM NICENUM*, Bach did not intend to provide a particularly individualized musical interpretation for each statement.

From the very beginning of the aria, one can sense a light, almost merry character. Bach composes in A major and therfore substitutes oboes d'amore, with their lower range, for regular oboes in this, the most sparsely scored piece in the *SYMBOLUM NICENUM*. Compared to the adjacent movements, the motives here are of a playful, relaxed character, and the treatment of the various motives is relatively uncomplicated. The use of identical music in mm. 2 and 3 is worthy of notice. So too is the oboe writing in the last three measures of the ritornello—on one hand because of the unison parts, and on the other, because the first and third measures here (mm. 10 and 12) are identical (ex. 101). In the

Ex. 101

treatment of the voice part as well, Bach proceeds more freely than he does in the other movements of the *SYMBOLUM NICENUM.* In mm. 29-36 (ex. 102), for example, he alters the order of the individual statements of the text in almost arbitrary fashion.

Ex. 102

Attempts have been made to base the interpretation of this aria on numerical relationships in the music. As interesting as this to some extent very complicated research is, it seems to have little to do with the purely musical structure of the movement, which quite obviously and deliberately avoids any profound interpretation of the text.

Nevertheless, the aria, whose 6/8 meter and rhythmic liveliness might well be sound-paintings for the activity of the life-giving Spirit, contains a number of details that are tied to the text in specific ways. First we have the word *vivificantem* ("giver of life"), whose motive structure in its first appearance in m. 16 is characterized by sixteenth notes. In the background of the basic eighth-note rhythm of the movement, these sixteenths seem like a rhythmic "animation." Here, for the illustration of the word *vivificantem,* Bach makes use of one of his favorite musical symbols: sixteenth notes on words having to do with "life" (ex. 103).

Ex. 103

Et in Spi-ri-tum san-ctum Do-mi-num et vi-vi-fi-can- - - - tem,

In the middle section of the aria one could see a substantially more-differentiated approach to the meaning of the text. Here Bach sets the words *qui cum Patre et filio simul adoratur et conglorificatur.* He depicts the similar and simultaneous worship of the Father, Son, and Holy Spirit in a passage beginning in m. 65, where the bass starts with a motive on the word *adoratur,* which is taken up similarly in the following measures by the two obbligato oboes (ex. 104). More significant than this place, which could also be viewed as purely structural

Ex. 104

imitation with no textual implications, is the continuo writing in mm. 69-72. Beginning with the C sharp in m. 69, the bass line builds upward chromatically, taking up once again the inversion of the passacaglia theme of the CRUCIFIXUS observed previously in the ET RESURREXIT. Viewed purely from the musical standpoint, this chromaticism, tied to the recollection of the text *Crucifixus etiam pro nobis,* clearly intensifies the setting. The tension built up in this way persists throughout the middle section of the aria. The canonic writing for bass and continuo that begins underneath the sustained C sharp in the oboe is noteworthy (ex. 105). In contrast with Bach's usual way of working, this structural peculiarity has no direct connection to the text, *qui locutus est per prophetas* ("who spoke by the prophets").

Ex. 105

To the end of the middle section, which is surprisingly similar to the third section of the ET RESURREXIT (ex. 106), Bach appends a modulation that could hardly be shorter or

Ex. 106

more insignificant (ex. 107). In terms of the thematic material, the treatment of motives, and

Ex. 107

the construction of periods of related measures, the da capo that starts in m. 93 corresponds exactly to the first section of the aria. Only at the end of the vocal part does there appear a passage not to be found in the earlier, analogous section: a more-elaborate, three-measure movement to the cadence. This use of da-capo form is unusual for two reasons. First, while the opening section of the aria deals with a long text containing two distinct ideas—*Et in Spiritum sanctum Dominum et vivificantem, qui cum Patre Filioque procedit* ("and in the Holy Spirit, the Lord and giver of life, who proceeds from the Father and the Son")—the da capo deals with a significantly shorter text that contains but a single idea—*Et unam sanctam catholicam et apostolicam ecclesiam* ("and in one holy catholic and apostolic church"). Second, if Bach had really wanted to do so, he could have differentiated the da capo from the beginning of the movement, to take into account the new and shorter texts, just as he did in the other da-capo movements of the *SYMBOLUM NICENUM* (ET IN UNUM DOMINUM and ET RESURREXIT), both of which also have different texts in the da-capo section. In addition, the da capo contains a number of strange divisions of the text as in mm. 105-109, with the emphasis on the word *et* in m. 107 (ex. 108).

Ex. 108

These observations raise some questions. Was the ET IN SPIRITUM SANCTUM truly originally composed for the *SYMBOLUM NICENUM*? What is the validity of such an hypothesis, based as it is on only the structure of the movement and a comparison with other movements of the *SYMBOLUM NICENUM*, with hardly any other evidence? Finally, regardless of whether or not the aria is an original composition, why is there no close relationship between music and text, when this is such a prominent characteristic of the other movements of the *SYMBOLUM NICENUM*?

In this aria, located between the concertato activity of the ET RESURREXIT and the profound interpretation of the CONFITEOR and the ET EXPECTO, Bach has intentionally created a movement that renounces interest in the text in favor of purely musical values.

The instrumentation of the continuo part is of considerable importance in the musical shaping of the aria. Bach does not specify the instruments to be used in the continuo group, expecting the normal complement of cello, contrabass, and organ. But the use of bassoon in place of cello seems not only possible, but interesting as well, since with this instrumentation, the piece acquires a very homogeneous character of sound that clearly sets it apart from the other cello-accompanied arias, such as the BENEDICTUS. In addition, the use of a wind instrument gives clarity to the voice leading of the continuo part. If it is too strenuous for a single player to assume the complete part, since two bassoonists must be present in any case for the QUONIAM TU SOLUS SANCTUS aria, the part can be divided up between them and passed back and forth. The use of bassoon in the continuo also underscores the playful and merry mood that should characterize the performance of the aria as a whole. This can best be assured by the use of a flowing tempo in which one feels the half-measure as the rhythmic pulse. The articulatory differentiation in the penultimate bar of the ritornello is delightful—though the notation of it in Bach's autograph score is not entirely clear. This deliberate differentiation between the two halves of the measure provides the opportunity to emphasize the musicianly element of the movement.

CONFITEOR UNUM BAPTISMA

The CONFITEOR begins the second of the pairs of choral movements that introduce and close Bach's setting of the *SYMBOLUM NICENUM*. In clear analogy to the opening movement of the *CREDO*, the CONFITEOR is also composed in the traditional style of sixteenth-century church music. As in the CREDO IN UNUM DEUM, this motet-like movement is suported by a continuo part that moves in quarter notes. Also as in that movement, in which a Gregorian *Credo* melody was used as the main theme, in the second half of the CONFITEOR Bach employs as a *cantus firmus* the Gregorian *confiteor* melody used in the Leipzig churches during his time. Despite these strong similarities, the structure of these two choral movements differs greatly. Using the bipartite structure of the text *Confiteor unum baptisma in remissionem peccatorum* ("I confess one baptism for the remission of sins"), Bach writes a movement in which the themes are initially stated and developed independently of each other. The first theme, which contains two statements of the word *confiteor*, is characterized by its rhythm, which is clearly derived from the textual declamation. In its normal form, its construction is exactly symmetrical (ex. 109). (This is not true of the modulated version which is used in the soprano II and tenor in the first section.) Before and after the central quarter-note F sharp in the third bar are grouped four and three notes, respectively, that exhibit the same intervallic content whether read forward or backward. The unequivocal meaning of the textual statement that finds expression in this structural pattern is further strengthened by the fact that Bach interprets the restatement of the word *confiteor* not as mere repetition, but through the broadening of the rhythm and the determined octave leap upward, as a reinforcement of its meaning.

Ex. 109

In the interest of the structure of the movement as a whole, Bach does not devote much time to treatment of this first theme. Thus, at the beginning, the theme is immediately introduced in close imitation—soprano I with soprano II, and alto with tenor—rather than alone. In this way, Bach is able to begin the second section, with its exposition of the second theme, as early as m. 16.

The rhythm of the second theme is also derived from the declamation of the text. The dominance of quarter notes, especially on the thrice-repeated initial pitch, gives the theme a motoric component that clearly contrasts it with the first theme. Bach sets this motoric rhythm in motion by moving an accompanying part—first the continuo and then the voice parts—from consonance to dissonance on the third of the repeated pitches (ex. 110). The dissonance between the third note of the theme and the accompanying part, usually a seventh, is subsequently resolved. Here too, a textual interpretation is related to a purely musical idea. In contrast to the first theme, the main emphasis in the second is at the beginning, on the word *remissionem* ("forgiveness"), and thereby, on the main point of the text: that forgiveness sets in motion the release of the tension brought about by sin (*peccatorum*). As in the case of the first theme, the second, three-and-one-half-measures in length, is not introduced alone. Rather, it appears successively in imitation in all parts, two measures apart. The development of the second theme is thus complete in m. 32, just sixteen measures after it began.

Ex. 110

From the immediate close imitation at the beginning of the third section, we can once again clearly discern Bach's intent to condense the structure. Even before the development of the second theme is complete in m. 32, he begins presenting the two themes simultaneously (m. 31). This coupling appears three times—first in the two sopranos, then in the alto and tenor, and finally in the sopranos again, but with the themes interchanged (ex. 111). Only when the two themes are combined is the full meaning of the textually subordinate musical structure revealed: the creed that is expressed in baptism signifies the simultaneous forgiveness of one's sins. It appears that Bach stresses the word *confiteor* and handles *unum baptisma* as comparatively secondary, so that he can shift somewhat the meaning of the thematic coupling: "I believe" means "you are forgiven." With this interpretation, one must certainly take into account the fact that Bach wanted to create similar musical settings for the CREDO IN UNUM DEUM at the beginning of his *SYMBOLUM NICENUM* and the CONFITEOR at the end. But even so, do we not see here the specifically Protestant, Lutheran thinking of Bach, for whom the concept of *sola fide* ("by faith alone") was crucial?

Ex. 111

Following this structural concentration the fugue continues with, at first, freer treatment of the themes. With m. 57 Bach begins increasingly to compress the setting once again (ex. 112). First he presents prominently the beginning of the first theme four times, with entries a measure apart, working up from the bass, through the tenor and second soprano, to the first soprano. A stretto on the second theme, with entries a half-bar apart in the bass, alto, and tenor, follows immediately in mm. 62-64. Continuing with free development, the voices, which Bach has taken into their high ranges, arrive at m. 69, where the quarter-note movement of the continuo comes to a halt in a pedal point.

Ex. 112

95

Following the ET INCARNATUS, the ET RESURREXIT, and the ET IN SPIRI-TUM SANCTUM, the CONFITEOR is the fourth movement of the *CREDO* in which Bach works with chromatic material related to the passacaglia theme of the CRUCI-FIXUS. In both mm. 16-18 of the continuo and mm. 64-67 of the continuo and vocal bass (counting the D sharps in the tenor and soprano I as the first note), Bach writes a chromatically stepwise-rising fourth—the inversion of the chromatic passacaglia theme. In mm. 65-68, this intentional analogy is underscored by the pitch repetitions in the continuo. In the CONFITEOR the chromatic line is associated only with the second half of the text, *in remissionem peccatorum*. This makes obvious the causal relationship between the chromatic "crucified for us" and the "forgiveness of sins" of the second theme.

After his profound interpretation of the CONFITEOR, marked by supreme mastery and ingenious extension of the contrapuntal technique of the traditional motet style, Bach now adds an objective component. He cites the Gregorian *cantus firmus*, first as a canon at the fifth between the bass and alto (mm. 73-88), written in half notes with entrances one measure apart, then in whole-note augmentation in the tenor (mm. 92-118). (The vocal parts and continuo from m. 73 to m. 123 are shown in ex. 113.) At the same time, the other

Ex. 113

voices present the thematic material that was worked over in the first half of the movement. It is obvious, however, that Bach did not place much importance on the treatment of these two themes in their original forms while he was dealing with the Gregorian *cantus firmus*. Only in the pause between the two citations of the *cantus firmus* (mm. 88-93) does the second theme appear intact once again. To be sure, the thematic material of the first half of the movement is always present in the form of the characteristic beginnings of the two themes. Too, the chromatic motive is included when the second soprano enters with the final quotation of the *cantus firmus* in the tenor (mm. 113-116). But the parts containing the *cantus firmus* are undoubtedly the most significant. Here Bach and his personal interpretation relinquish the place of importance to the objective affirmation of the Gregorian quotation.

After the close of the final *cantus-firmus* section, the piece arrives at the key of G major, the subdominant of the D major Bach needs for the beginning of the *adagio* section. If he had wished, he could thus have started here with the new section. But instead, he expands the modulation and occupies himself once again with the text *in remissionem peccatorum*. Especially because of the unusual writing for the alto in mm. 121 and 122, the word *peccatorum* assumes the place of prominence. Bach paid special attention to this word at only one other place earlier in the CONFITEOR. Carried by the chromatic line of the continuo and vocal bass, and entering on a high-lying syncopation in the tenor in m. 67, the word *peccatorum* in mm. 67-69 dominates the cadence that concludes the previous section. If one considers this place as an interpretation of the text, the entrance of *peccatorum* possesses an almost triumphant character: through the act of Christ's redemption symbolized by the chromatic bass line, the forgiveness of sin becomes an incontestable certainty. But now, in the final measures of the CONFITEOR, *peccatorum* appears in an entirely different way. Bach imparts to it a somber expression, just as he does when he deals with the idea of sin so frequently in his cantatas and Passions. One is almost inclined to relate the immediately following text, *Et expecto resurrectionem mortuorum* ("and I look for the resurrection of the dead"), with its implicit portent of the Last Judgement, to the characterization given *peccatorum* in mm. 121 and 122. The character of the passage is perhaps well explained by a portion of the text to cantata BWV 199, *Mein Herze schwimmt im Blut* (My Heart Swims in Blood)—only one of many possible examples from Bach's cantatas—"... and I must hide myself before Thee, before whom the angels themselves cover their faces."

It is of the utmost importance to the shaping of the piece up to this point to render the two initial themes so firmly and distinctly that the textual clarity of this structurally dense movement is ensured. The determination of the first theme can be projected by the use of marcato articulation based on stressed consonants. Along with this textual accentuation, it is important to keep in mind the linear component of the music leading to the repetition of the word confiteor. *On the other hand, the second theme, set to the words* in remissionem peccatorum, *should have a shorter articulation in order to keep clearly audible the pitch repetition at the beginning. With this deliberate differentiation between themes, it should be possible to hear them both clearly when they appear together at the beginning of the double fugue. After the intensity of the beginning of the movement, which underscored the dogmatic character of the CONFITEOR, the second fugato can begin with some restraint. The structural compression created by the gradual addition of the voices must be comple-*

mented by a deliberate intensification of sound. After the first climaxes at the coupling of the two themes and the subsequent, careful release of tension, one can see in the structure of the movement the need for another intensification. The cadential measures that precede the pedal point are established as a climax by the preceding strettos on the first and second themes, the ascent of the voiceleading, and the chromatic writing in the bass, which creates harmonic intensification.

The Gregorian cantus firmus *assumes the place of importance in the next portion of the movement. Sung forte and marcato, it must always be clearly heard, and the other elements of the setting must be subordinate to it. This can be most easily achieved by reducing the number of performers on the parts that do not have the Gregorian theme. On the other hand, it would be sensible to ensure a good balance between the bass and alto in the canon at the fifth by adding tenors to the alto part. Although the thematic material of the first part of the movement is secondary to the* cantus firmus *here, it must never become just a vague background. It must be given an articulatory vitality that never permits the rhythmically active component of the movement to be lost.*

Bach sets the text *Et expecto resurrectionem mortuorum* twice—first in a twenty-four-measure adagio, then in the closing vivace e allegro. (See ex. 114 for the complete score to

Ex. 114

the adagio.) Aside from the introductory, four-measure *kyrie* that precedes the fugue on the same text, this is the only text in the entire Mass that Bach treats in two, contrasting ways. The significance thus given to the words *et expecto resurrectionem mortuorum* is underscored by the fact that Bach did not consider possible two settings of the text *Et incarnatus est* (see p. 79) and therefore reworked the duet to omit that text when he decided to set it as a new choral movement.

The most salient characteristic of the twenty-four-measure adagio is its harmonic instability. Bach's modulations from the initial D major are so constant and extreme—for example, within the duration of one measure in mm. 124 and 125, he goes from D major to E-sharp minor—that it is very difficult for the listener to establish any sense of harmonic orientation. An examination of the harmony, rhythm, and motives Bach assigns to the individual words in the first section of the adagio (mm. 123-137) shows the word *expecto* characterized by B-flat and its related keys as well as long-held notes; no particular motive is associated with it, however. By contrast, the word *resurrectionem* is usually tied to D major or its related keys. Too, its rhythm consists primarily of quarter notes, and there are two distinct motives associated with it: the diatonically rising, scalar fourth found, for example, in the first sopranos in mm. 130 and 131; and the broken triads in the tenor and bass, as, for example, in m. 134. For the word *mortuorum*, Bach mainly uses diminished chords (as in mm. 132 and 133), or minor chords derived from the major-key tendency of the movement by flatting the third (as in the first soprano in m. 131). There is no consistent rhythmic treatment of the word, though the whole notes of the first soprano from m. 132 and the approach to the cadence in mm. 135-137 produce a slowing and calming of the earlier quarter-note movement. There is no perceptible motivic representation of the word *mortuorum*.

In attempting to comprehend what Bach achieves in these few bars in terms of textual interpretation, one must start with the fact that his use of modulation destroys the initial key of D major. This key is symbolic of the resurrection: D major is the key of the ET RESURREXIT as well as the triumphant ET EXPECTO, which speaks of the resurrection of the dead. Thus, in this treatment of the *et expecto* text within the CONFITEOR, B flat and its related keys—especially the darkened E-flat-minor tonality of m. 125—signify a backing away from the certain faith in the resurrection. The long-held notes, which Bach had used as his musical symbol for the expression of "waiting" since his earliest cantata, *Aus der Tiefe rufe ich, Herr, zu dir* (BWV 131), are followed by the rhythmically active quarter-note movement on the word *resurrectionem*. Both the D-major tendency in individual groups of voices and the motives that anticipate the next movement (the tenor part in m. 134 corresponds precisely to the tenor in m. 7 of the allegro e vivace, and the diatonically ascending fourth in mm. 130 and 131 appears in embellished form in the tenor part in mm. 87-89 of the allegro) permit one to perceive the vague outline of the resurrection, but it is never made tangible by means of a cadence. The word *mortuorum*, to which each voice descends after the word *resurrectionem,* characterizes the conclusion of this part of the movement by its low tessitura, symbolic of the kingdom of the dead.

With the A-major chord in m. 137, Bach reaches the dominant of D major and could immediately begin the vivace e allegro. But instead, he writes an extension and begins again with the *et expecto* text. The first three notes in the soprano I are in F major—once again Bach uses a B-flat-related key, just as he did in the previous section for the interpretation of the same text. But then, in m. 139, he changes the C^2 in the soprano I to its enharmonic equivalent, B sharp[1], and with the remaining voices, modulates to the bright, sharp key of C-sharp major—in deliberate contrast to the E-flat-minor of the previous section. This is the sole place in the entire Mass in which Bach uses enharmonic change. Chapter 15, verses 50-57 of Paul's first letter to the Corinthians ("... but we shall all be changed. ...") come instantly to mind as a basis for the interpretation of this section. In the transformation of C to B sharp, the essence and musical function of the note change, although the sound remains the same. Surely this is intended to be a musical synonym for the expectation of the resurrection as an event that does not destroy reality, but rather, transcends it and changes its nature.

Following the symbolic ascending motives in all voices on the word *resurrectionem*, the emphasis of the final bars of the adagio is on the idea of *mortuorum* ("of the dead").

Earlier, in m. 136, on the same word, it was notable that the alto was taken above the two soprano parts and made the highest voice. Now, in m. 144, Bach does the same with the tenor part, taking it as high as the higher of the two soprano parts. Here we have a representation of the resurrection of the dead: that which lay at the bottom rises to the top. The seventh chords in mm. 144 and 145 correspond to the diminished chords seen earlier with the same text (mm. 132 and 133). The particular character of these chords as not harmonically independent, but rather as harmonic structures in need of resolution, is used here as a depiction of the expectation of the resurrection, which is prepared in the last bar of the adagio by the motion of the continuo from A major to D major, and becomes reality with the beginning of the vivace e allegro.

The performance of the adagio must be characterized by the utmost restraint in terms of dynamics. This restraint should also rule out any use of accentuation and any attempt to make rhythmic activity perceptible. The resulting quality of sound portrays the state of waiting and the blind groping for what one can indeed suspect, but cannot grasp. Certainly, the previously observed, fleeting D-major glimpse of the resurrection on the word resurrectionem *should be audible, but should not in any way suggest the reality of the word. The choir can complement the unreal dimension of the text by the use of an almost whispered diction.*

Implied in the use of the stile-antico *in Bach's time was the* colla-voce *playing of instruments, and Bach followed this practice, as in the* stile-antico *movements from cantatas 2, 38, 64, and others. When Carl Philipp Emanuel Bach reorchestrated his father's* SYMBOLUM NICENUM *for a 1786 performance, he provided* colla-voce *string and wind parts for the* CONFITEOR. *It would be most effective to adopt a modification of this idea in modern performances. Strings and winds might play up to m. 123/2. The winds could then be omitted in order to emphasize the restrained character of the adagio section. The use of string accompaniment would have the added benefit of assisting the choir in maintaining precise intonation in this difficult passage.*

It would seem logical to provide similar colla-voce *accompaniment to the CREDO IN UNUM DEUM, and in C.P.E. Bach's reorchestration, he did so, using winds. That movement, however, contains two obbligato violin parts, and the addition of* colla-voce *winds would damage the balance of the seven-part texture.*

ET EXPECTO

It has been shown that in the first of the pairs of choral movements that frame the *SYMBOLUM NICENUM,* the CREDO IN UNUM DEUM and the PATREM OMNIPOTENTEM, Bach acquired the second movement by reworking a chorus from a cantata. He uses the same procedure in the closing pair of choral movements: the ET EXPECTO is a major revision of the large-scale choral movement from the 1728 cantata for the inauguration of the Leipzig town council, *Gott, man lobet dich in der Stille,* BWV 120 (God, Man Praises Thee in the Stillness of Zion). The fact that Bach took the trouble to expand the original from four to five voices shows quite obviously that he felt it impossible for the five-voice CONFITEOR to lead into a four-voice ET EXPECTO. His compositional skill here was so exceptional that only by a direct comparison with the score of the cantata can one detect the four voices of the original. For example, in mm. 40-49, he retained the order of entries in the fugato—alto, soprano, tenor, and bass—but composed the soprano II entrance just before the bass so naturally that one gets the impression that this compression was a part of the original design of the movement (ex. 115).

Ex. 115

With all of the Mass movements that were taken from cantatas, one is struck by the painstaking care that Bach took to find movements that corresponded to the Mass text in terms of textual content, motives, and compositional structure. In none of the parody movements, however, is there as close a relationship between the text of the Mass and the music originally conceived for the text of a cantata, as there is in the ET EXPECTO. This is true even to the extent that in the first section at the very least, the motives and structure more directly reflect the text of the Mass, *Et expecto resurrectionem mortuorum*: ("and I look for the resurrection of the dead") than the text of the cantata, *Jauchzet ihr erfreuten Stimmen*, ("Rejoice, ye gladdened voices"). The fact that the orchestral introduction to the cantata movement does not begin at forte immediately, but rather reaches its full volume only after a composed crescendo, no doubt has its basis in the preceding movement on the text "God, man praises thee in the stillness of Zion," from whose chamber-music-like instrumentation the tutti of the orchestra gradually develops. The orchestral introduction, which appears in both works (though simultaneously with the choir in the Mass) makes far more sense in the context of the Mass than it did in the cantata. The fanfare motive that ascends from the low range, the timpani that enter before the trumpets, and the intensification of the opening measures produced by the progressive upward movement of the setting and the constantly expanding instrumentation—all of these depict excitingly the jubilant vision of the resurrection that breaks out of the somber final bars of the adagio (ex. 116). Even

more immediate is the connection between the Mass text and the music to which it is set in mm. 25-32, where the timpani function soloistically and not just as the bass instruments of the trumpet group. It is true that this soloistic timpani writing, which is so rarely found in Bach's music, appears in the cantata as well, but there it has no specific role in the interpretation of the text, "Rejoice, ye gladdened voices." In the Mass, on the other hand, the constant alternation of the fanfare-like figuration in the orchestra with the timpani entrances can be seen as symbolic of the sound of the last trumpet and the quaking of the earth on the day of resurrection (ex. 117).

The cantata model also provides the motive that Bach introduces in the middle of the movement in m. 41, on the word *resurrectionem*. He uses it as well on the word "amen" in the last section in m. 87 and for the development of the following fugatos. It owes its ascending-spiral form to the cantata text, *Steiget bis zum Himmel 'nauf* ("climb up to heaven") (ex. 118). From the comparisons in ex. 118, it is clear that this motive, which

Ex. 118

originated with and reflects the cantata text, retains its original meaning in its reuse within the Mass. The fugato theme on *resurrectionem* embodies the gesture of the "climb to heaven" in the context of the resurrection of the dead. The meanings of both the cantata and Mass texts—the "climb to heaven" of the "gladdened voices" as well as the awareness of the upward-thrusting resurrection of the dead—are included in the amen.

By the time Bach introduces the concluding section of the movement with the "amen" theme, he has really already completed setting the *et expecto* text. After the trumpet interjections in mm. 77-82 (ex. 119), which break into the setting like rays of light from a world to come, Bach compresses the tension up to the cadence before the amen with the entries of the chorus a half-measure apart on the words *et vitam* and the immediately following unison writing for the timpani-supported trumpet choir. The cadence (mm. 86-87), introduced in signal-like fashion by the tenor, triumphantly underscores the message of the text.

Thus, the amen that follows now is not only the conclusion of the ET EXPECTO, but bound as it is to the prospect of eternal life, it is also the conclusion of the entire affirmation of the *Credo*. From the paucity of forces of its beginning in the tenor and viola, the amen develops itself by the continuous addition of every available group within the ensemble, building in intensity by the upward voiceleading to the cadence in the last three measures. Here, as the climax of the previous development, Bach brings the choral voices together homophonically on the text *venturi saeculi. Amen*. Through the eighth notes in the high trumpets and the sixteenth notes in the winds and first violin, he gives this confirmation of the text an extraordinarily vital—and with the short-held final chord, an ecstatic—interpretation (ex. 120). With this short final chord and the precisely notated rests that end the ET EXPECTO, and thus, the entire setting of the *SYMBOLUM NICENUM*, it seems as if Bach quite deliberately wanted to avoid any dissipation of tension. He thus builds a bridge to the next text to be set, which like no other describes the reality of *vitam venturi saeculi* ("the life of the world to come"): *Sanctus Dominus Deus sabaoth* ("Holy is the Lord, God of hosts").

The musical realization of the allegro e vivace must be possessed of extraordinary vitality and must, in many ways, have an almost ecstatic dimension. This indicates the necessity for a relentless dynamic intensity and a vehement grasp of the intensifications that ensue from the structure of the piece. Whereas in the other movements of the Mass the trumpets have had to play relatively lightly, so that the other winds might be heard, here they could become progressively stronger and more dramatic. The timpani as well should play the solo passage with a strength and intensity not heard in the work up to this point. Still, the texture of the movement must remain transparent. Sustained chords must not obscure the clarity of the fugato developments (mm. 69-77, for example), and high, non-thematic trumpet chords must not conceal the low-lying eighth-note motion (mm. 55-56). Too, the articulation of both the choir and orchestra should possess intensity throughout, and therefore must avoid both a gentle legato and the playful informality of a too-short staccato.

SANCTUS

The *SANCTUS* is the oldest portion of the *B-Minor Mass*. Bach wrote it in 1723, about ten years before the settings of the *KYRIE* and *GLORIA*, and more than twenty years before completing the Mass with the *SYMBOLUM NICENUM* and the other missing movements. The *SANCTUS* originated as communion music for the Christmas service and was probably first heard on December 25, 1723.

This fact explains why the scoring of the piece differs from that of the other portions of the Mass. In addition to the usual scoring for a four-part string group and three timpani-supported trumpets, Bach employs here not just two, but three oboes. This is not surprising, since cantata BWV 63, *Christen ätzet diesen Tag* (*Christians, Etch This Day*)—intended to be performed in the same service in which the *SANCTUS* received its first performance—is likewise scored for three oboes.

The choral scoring, on the other hand, is unusual. If one disregards *Der Streit zwischen Phoebus und Pan* (BWV 201: *The Quarrel Between Phoebus and Pan*), in two movements of which the six soloists are brought together chorally under the names of their specific characters, the *SANCTUS* is the sole piece in which Bach utilizes a six-part chorus. The vocal setting, which is in six true parts without doubling, is partially chordal, partially polyphonic. In the first part of the movement, Bach repeatedly removes three, in each case different, combinations of voices from the six-voice texture and contrasts them with the tutti. Twice, for three bars at a time, the three highest and three lowest voices alternate in double-choir fashion. In the fugue as well, after the six-voice exposition, measures for a reduced number of voices alternate with entrances of the vocal tutti.

The numbers three and six are clearly prominent in the structure of this movement. As suggested by several scholars, it is possible that Bach intended these numbers to function symbolically. In particular, the number six may be related to the passage in Isaiah's prophesy (6:2 and 3) that includes the text of the *SANCTUS*: "Above him stood the seraphim; each had six wings: with two he covered his face, and with two he covered his feet, and with two he flew. And one called to the other and said: 'Holy, holy, holy is the Lord of hosts; heaven and earth are full of Thy glory.'" This possibility and several others could be examined in great detail, but in the final analysis, they do not contribute to an understanding of the performance of the movement, and thus will not be discussed further here.

The basic structure of the first portion of the movement adheres to the principles of polychoral composition. The trumpets, oboes, strings, and chorus remain together in groups for the most part, exchanging motives that differ in their rhythmic contours but remain individually unaltered. Aside from a single five-bar fugato period, during which the instruments sometimes play with the choir, there is but seldom any doubling of the voices. In the fugue also, the tendency toward the use of orchestral instruments in groups is still in evidence, although here it is natural that *colla-parte* scoring predominates, precluding true polychoral writing.

Only in a few of the other movements of the Mass are there sections in which individual groups are lifted from the ensemble as a whole and set against each other. But in neither the

ET IN TERRA PAX fugue nor the CUM SANCTO SPIRITU nor the OSANNA are the principles of polychoral composition and the group concerto the dominant elements of structure. This throws light upon Bach's expressive intent to reserve them for his setting of the text *Sanctus, sanctus, sanctus, Dominus Deus sabaoth*. The spatial dimension of the music, a characteristic of polychoral writing since its beginning, makes this movement of the Mass stand out from all the others.

Bach divides the complete text of the *Sanctus* into two sections. The motivic structure of the setting of the words *Sanctus, sanctus, sanctus Dominus Deus sabaoth* is characterized by five different rhythmic figures (ex. 121). Each of the subdivided rhythms here (c and d)

Ex. 121

is to be understood within a triplet context. The sixteenth note and the four thirty-second notes should sound on the third eighth note of the triplet figure. The lone eighth note should be held only as a triplet eighth, but the one preceding the four thirty-second notes must be held as two triplet eighths. Each of these basic rhythmic figures possesses its own, individual expressive value. The quarter-note motive gives the movement a character of majestic grandeur—especially when combined with the octave leap in the bass. The triplet eighth notes, which usually occur in a series and are developed linearly, become bearers of a solemn, but enthusiastic expression. The sixteenth-note and thirty-second-note rhythms that are performed within the triplet context counterbalance the linear tendency of the uniformly flowing triplets and give them an upbeat component as well as providing the entire setting with an underlying, pulsing momentum. The single eighth notes function largely to intensify the sound.

Bach begins his working over of this basic rhythmic and motivic material at the beginning of the movement with three cries of *sanctus*, followed by the entire text in mm. 5 and 6 (ex. 122). This six-measure period is immediately repeated twice, with an exchange of

119

motives, but the same structure is retained. The measures that follow are characterized by three chords, each sustained in the five upper voices for two measures. The bass parts of the chorus and orchestra have a contrasting part that acts rather like a *cantus firmus*, the majesty of which is characterized by the octave motion of the scales that stride downward into the low range (ex. 123). After two transitional measures, during which the octave motion

Ex. 123

in the bass and continuo comes to a halt with a cadence, come the "double-choir" bars discussed above, in which a high and a low chorus alternately exchange the triplet and quarter-note figures (ex. 124). With the end of the section containing the choral chords (m.

Ex. 124

23), Bach starts reducing the intensity of the orchestral setting. In mm. 28 and 29, he relaxes the tension in the choral parts as well, via the downward motion of the voices. The following polyphonic structure of the choral setting (ex. 125) immediately becomes the starting point for an intensification characterized by the five-and-one-half measures of upward-striding octaves in the continuo, and the continuous increase of density that leads to the trumpet entrance and the return of the sustained chords on the word *sanctus* (m. 35). The three

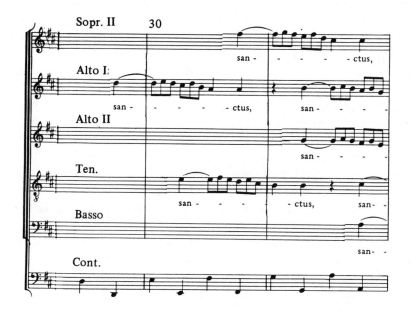

segments that conclude this section of the *SANCTUS* repeat the structure of the preceding periods, but they intensify it in that the instruments that previously had only the basic, quarter-note rhythm, now enter into the triplet movement—the first trumpet in mm. 39 and 40, and the continuo in mm. 44-46.

The inner tension built by the intensity of sound and constantly present in the first section of the movement is released in the fugue on the words *Pleni sunt coeli et terra gloria ejus* ("heaven and earth are full of Your glory"). Bach desired a contrast here: instead of the seventeen-part texture used up to now, one voice begins alone; instead of the carefully balanced and symbol-laden rhythms of the first section, the rhythmic character of the motivic material is light and lively. In addition, the fugue is not strictly constructed. The doubling of the subject in thirds and tenths, which Bach employs as he usually does as an intensifying device in the concluding section of the fugue, appears as early as the first exposition of the subject in the alto I and soprano II, beginning in m. 66, and in the bass and tenor in m. 72.

One can see in the six-measure length of the fugue subject a relationship to the periods of the same length at the beginning of the movement. The most prominent aspect of the subject is its rhythm. Following the repeated notes at the beginning of the subject, the sixteenth-note motion on the word *gloria* brings with it a certain momentum that clarifies the hemiolic counter-rhythm of the last two measures of the subject (ex. 126, mm. 52 and 53). The immediately following counter subject in the tenor, with its uninterrupted sixteenth-note coloratura, demonstrates even more clearly than the subject itself Bach's desire to write a virtuosic, "play-fugue". Many details of the movement demonstrate this intention.

Ex. 126

as for example, when in m. 70 Bach playfully alters the previous sixteenth-note motion of the countersubject (here in a duet in sixths between the soprano I and the alto II) into virtuosic thirty-second notes, and when he ornaments the alto II in the preceding bar (ex. 127).

Ex. 127

After the close of the exposition, Bach introduces in m. 78 a new, fanfare-like motive that dominates the passages between the three entrances of the subject in the tenor and the first soprano (mm. 87, 98, and 113). Sometimes the motive appears in its complete form (ex. 128), and at other times, only the first four notes are heard.

Ex. 128

The movement acquires the character of a playful concerto from the contrasts between the individual groups of voices that are always emerging from the vocal ensemble in alternation, as well as from the tutti writing for the orchestra. Only with the beginning of the next exposition of the subject in m. 119 does the setting become more intense as the orchestra plays all the choral parts and intensifies several places by playing in parallel thirds.

For the last two episodes that are once again constructed from the first four sixteenth notes of the motive discussed above (ex. 124), Bach reserved two compositional techniques that he had not used in the fugue up to this point. In the section beginning in m. 137, he composes *per choros*—for individual choirs—constructing the orchestral setting so that a double-choir effect results between the oboes and strings. The climax of this passage is the stretto on the fugue subject between the soprano I and the trumpet (mm. 147 and 148) that springs forth from the virtuosic bass coloratura. The technique he uses for the last episode,

beginning in m. 153, is a textbook-perfect example of a composed crescendo. All of the parts here begin in a relatively low range and move constantly upward for five measures. The intensification of sound is underscored by the chromaticizing of the bass part, and especially, by the counter-accent rhythm of the violin I and trumpet I. The development of this crescendo culminates with the reentry of the trumpet-and-timpani-supported motive in the bass (m. 158) that had characterized the episodes earlier in the fugue. Here it is followed immediately by the final statement of the fugue subject (ex 130).

Fine

The performance of the first part of the SANCTUS must be possessed of great intensity of sound and rhythm, but this intensity should never degenerate into sheer massiveness and hectic activity. Despite the fact that fullness of sound is desired, one must also pay attention to clarity of texture, especially in the part writing for the three oboes. For example, one can deliberately hold back the sustained chords in the five upper voice parts in order to clear the way for the other parts, particularly the bass. In order to make a contrast with the first part of the movement and to leave room for further intensification, the fugue on the words pleni sunt coeli *should begin thoroughly relaxed.*

The eighth notes at the beginning of the fugue subject must be articulated non legato; the following downbeats, which already possess natural stress, should not receive additional accent. At the conclusion of the crescendos that arise from the structure of the movement, the new sections of the fugue must begin in a relaxed manner once again. Only from the background of this relaxation will the full extent of the great climaxes at the conclusion of the fugue be clearly heard.

When in Bach's latter **years** he separated this setting of the *Sanctus* from its ties to performance within a specific church service and placed it within the larger context of a musical setting of the complete text of the Mass, this did not signify a renunciation of the special connection of the movement to the communion portion of the Mass celebration. Rather, it broadened the scope of the association. It was shown earlier, in the examination of the last measure of the *SYMBOLUM NICENUM*, that Bach avoided creating any real sense of finality by making the final chord just a quarter note long and completing the measure with rests. In addition, this conclusion lacks the words *fine* and *Soli Deo gloria* that appear at the ends of the other major sections of the Mass, such as the *GLORIA*. It thus appears as if Bach deliberately intended to continue in the *SANCTUS* the tension he had built up in the last section of the immediately preceding *ET EXPECTO*. Understood in this way, the *SANCTUS* is the vision foreseen in the hope and expectation of the *et vitam venturi*. Here Bach formulates the sublimity and infinitude of the hymn of praise that sounds throughout eternity without the assistance of mankind. With the beginning of the fugue, an idea seems to break away from this enraptured vision withheld from human experience—an idea that describes the reality of the eternal hymn of praise for all of creation, for *coeli et terrae*. After the first exposition of the fugue subject, the text *pleni sunt coeli . . .* acquires a new theme that with its fanfare-like motive, possesses the character of an invitation. The subsequent *OSANNA* picks up both this summons and the theme itself and, with its enthusiastic unison beginning, symbolizes the joining of mankind in the heavenly hymn of praise.

OSANNA-BENEDICTUS-OSANNA

The subsequent text of the Mass, with its threefold declaration of praise (*Osanna in excelsis—Benedictus qui venit in nomine Domini—Osanna in excelsis*: "Hosanna in the highest—Blessed is He who comes in the name of the Lord—Hosanna in the Highest") is so significant that Bach could not have permitted its setting to be inferior to the *SANCTUS*. Yet how could he manage this, after the brilliantly conceived and executed setting of that movement? He succeeds through his handling of the scoring. Whereas Bach reserved for the *SANCTUS* the special scoring for six-part choir and three oboes that makes that movement stand out from all others, in the OSANNA he returns to normal scoring, but expands it to the limit. The division of the choir into eight parts and the reentry of the flutes give the twenty-part OSANNA the distinction of being the piece with the greatest number of parts in the entire Mass setting. Then follows the greatest possible contrast: Bach's use of just three parts in the BENEDICTUS represents the fewest number of parts to be found in any movement of the Mass.

OSANNA

Bach's setting of the OSANNA is a reworking of the opening choral movement to the secular cantata *Preise dein Glücke, gesegnetes Sachsen* (BWV 215: *Praise Your Good Fortune, Blessed Saxony*). Aside from the large-scale scoring that Bach wanted for the OSANNA and which was already to be found in the cantata movement, Bach's reason for using this particular movement lies in the close similarity of the principal motive of the cantata movement to the motive that appears for the first time in the bass part in m. 78 of the *pleni sunt coeli* fugue (ex. 131). Bach begins the OSANNA differently from the cantata model,

Ex. 131

however, by omitting the extensive instrumental introduction and having the eight-part chorus begin alone, in unison, on the textual and musical motto shown in ex. 131c. Then one instrumental group after another—continuo, flutes, oboes, violins, and trumpets—enters on the same motto, with each entrance just a measure apart, propelling the structure of sound inexorably into the twenty-part climax in mm. 7-10.

The contrapuntal section that begins in m. 15 is of amazing architectural clarity. First Bach develops a coloratura fugato motive (ex. 132) in the four voices of the first choir. In the

Ex. 132

continuation of this fugato development, the instruments present the opening motto in unison (m. 23/3), followed by three unison statements of the same in the second choir, two measures apart. This twenty-three-measure fugato section is followed by another of precisely the same length, in which the roles of the two choirs are reversed. On the upbeat to m. 39 the second choir begins the development of the coloratura fugato motive, then the orchestra takes up the unison motto, followed by the first choir. Subsequent to these two precisely corresponding segments of the movement, Bach begins a section (m. 62/3) in which the fugato motive, heard up to this time only in the eight voices of the two choirs, moves through all parts of the ensemble, with each entrance two measures apart. The motive appears first in bass I, then tenor I, alto I, soprano I, soprano II, alto II, tenor II, bass II, winds and strings, and finally the trumpets (ex. 133). The climax of this contrapuntal compression and natural, composed crescendo is the entrance of the timpani on the upbeat to m. 85.

The next eight measures are characterized by the further development of the motto in concertato fashion in the first violins, first oboe, and both flutes, all of which play in unison (ex. 134). The further concertato development of the fugato motive extends for another

Ex. 134

O - san-na, o san-na,

eight measures (ex. 135). The syncopations of the first trumpet intensify the next three bars,

Ex. 135

in which the two choirs first alternate, then come together in eight parts to conclude this concertato section (ex. 136). After bringing the entire ensemble into use in concertato

Ex. 136

fashion in this section, and before beginning the orchestral postlude, Bach produces a conclusion of extreme contrast by setting vocal passages marked "piano" against "forte" blocks of tutti sound.

I have discussed the structure of the OSANNA in such analytical detail because I believe that the special dimension of the movement, with its location in the Mass text—following the settings of the *SANCTUS* and *pleni sunt coeli*—can be fully appreciated only in this way. Many commentators have stated that the movements from the OSANNA through the DONA NOBIS PACEM do not match the high quality of the preceding movements. I cannot agree with this opinion. It seems to me as if, after the visionary *SANCTUS*, the beginning of the OSANNA depicts the emotional uniting of the terrestrial and heavenly hymns of praise. The enthusiastic choral beginning summons out one instrumental group after another until the twenty-part climax; the two opposing four-voice choirs reflect the visionary image of the two seraphim. When, after the intensity of sound at the outset, the fugato development begins with once-again reduced voicing, the merely emotional expression of the text is transformed into a deliberately formulated declaration that is passed one voice to another and is taken up by the instruments after all of the vocal resources have been exhausted. The climax in m. 85, marked by the timpani entrance, finally signifies the moment when the vocal motto, now an independent, obbligato instrumental part, comes to dominate the enthusiastic vitality of the entire movement. The four measures marked "piano" (mm. 104/3-108/2) seem almost like a reverberation of the preceding tutti sound, before the closing measures of the vocal section underscore the words *Osanna in excelsis* with the forte of the ensemble and the upward-moving trumpets. It is logical that the movement should end as it does with a purely instrumental section, given the previously observed transition from vocal to instrumental dominance within the movement. The full proclamation of the movement is brought together here, when analogously with the vocal beginning, the strings and woodwinds play in unison, and the trumpets play in their high range in symbolism of the text *in excelsis* (ex. 137).

Ex. 137

After creating the forward-thrusting intensity that must characterize the beginning of the *OSANNA*, the most important task in the performance of the movement is to clarify the structure of the various fugato sections. In order to emphasize each entrance in the fugato, it will be necessary to deliberately hold back the other parts of the ensemble. Above all, the playful, chamber-music component of the setting must stand in the foreground at the beginning of the fugato development and be the determinant of the articulation and dynamics. The eight-voice fugato development, with the immediately following taking over of the motive by the instruments, should be accompanied by a corresponding crescendo that culminates with the climactic entrance of the timpani in m. 84. The following section, which incorporates the full forces of the ensemble, must be performed with vitality, but must be balanced so that the structurally determined dominance of the instruments is also clearly audible.

In the discussion of the ET EXPECTO, it was quite apparent how forcibly the end of that movement led into the *SANCTUS* and made plain the direct connection between the two. An even more intimate connection exists between the *pleni sunt coeli* fugue that closes the setting of the *SANCTUS*, and the beginning of the OSANNA. In addition to the identical motives that tie the movements together, an immediate continuation is suggested by the choral-unison beginning and the lack of an instrumental introduction. An identical tempo for both movements would emphasize this relationship. In this way, the tension is not simply cut off, and the unity of the individual sections of the Mass is stressed.

BENEDICTUS

Whereas in Bach's setting of the OSANNA he used the largest-scale scoring of the entire Mass, in the subsequent movement, the BENEDICTUS, he used the fewest number of parts. The movement is written for just three parts—tenor, continuo, and one obbligato instrument. Quite obviously, it was Bach's desire to follow the supremely majestic display of the OSANNA, whch he had intensified to the limit, with a setting of the text *Benedictus qui venit in nomine Domini* ("Blessed is He who comes in the name of the Lord") that would be possessed of meditative restraint. Bach did not specify what obbligato instrument he desired. While the range of the part indicates that one might use either violin or flute, it also suggests the flute as the better choice. In Bach's solo violin parts, he customarily made use of the entire lower register of the instrument, but here the lowest note is only D, a full fifth above the lowest note of the violin. It would thus be possible to play the aria without using the G string at all. The D is quite close, however, to the lowest pitch available on the Baroque flute (C). The flute also seems more capable than the violin of producing the special expression peculiar to this aria. A comparison with the St. Matthew Passion strengthens this conclusion. Just as the BENEDICTUS falls between the two OSANNA choruses in the Mass, the Passion aria *Aus Liebe will mein Heiland sterben* lies between the two identical *Lass ihn kreuzigen* choruses. The flute is the obbligato instrument in this aria, which, presenting a distinct contrast to the surrounding, dramatic *turbae*, was conceived as a meditative pause within the Passion story. Notwithstanding all of the differences between the two movements, the expressive natures of the instrumental obbligato parts are quite similar (ex. 138).

Ex. 138

The structure of the obbligato part, with its constant alternation of sixteenth notes, sixteenth-note triplets, thirty-second notes, and numerous suspensions, imparts an improvisatory character to the instrumental setting (ex. 139).

Ex. 139

In contrast to the triplet figuration that dominates the purely instrumental sections, the tenor part is characterized by eighth notes and sixteenth notes; there is no triplet movement. It is interesting to observe how Bach develops the beginning of the vocal part out of the beginning of the instrumental introduction, despite the basic difference in rhythmic structure between the two (ex. 140).

Ex. 140

The movement acquires its tranquil expression from the eighth-note and sixteenth-note motion as well as from the often-melismatic writing for the tenor. This is underscored by Bach's use of sixteenth-note figuration in the obbligato part in those sections where the voice sings (ex. 141). Here the triplets merely provide bridges between vocal periods. An

Ex. 141

expression of meditative restraint prevails throughout the movement, emphasized by the harmonic digression on the first beat of m. 45, which takes the place of the anticipated cadence, and the "lonely" conclusion of the tenor part, not even supported by the continuo (ex. 142, m. 48).

Ex. 142

The distribution of the text in the tenor part is noteworthy. The many repetitions of individual statements are not developed logically and are in some cases so haphazard (ex. 143) that one might suspect the aria to have originally possessed another text. If one also

Ex. 143

takes into account the character of the script in Bach's score, which is more suggestive of a copy than a new composition, it becomes plausible that the BENEDICTUS, like the two other movements following the OSANNA, is a parody the prototype of which is unknown.

A very tranquil tempo and above all, a restraint of dynamics are necessary in order to bring out the meditative restraint of the BENEDICTUS. Even the high passages for the tenor must enter into this restrained expression. In the purely instrumental sections, a judicious freedom of tempo would emphasize the improvisatory character of the obbligato part. Only the cello and organ should be used on the continuo part. Even though there are several notes in the tenor part that go lower than the continuo if the contrabass is omitted (strictly speaking, producing an inversion of the chord), the use of cello alone assists in bringing out the restraint and relaxed mood of the aria. Since the cello will be the only continuo instrument besides the organ, it must support the setting with linear expressivity, notwithstanding the basic restraint of the movement.

The restraint of the BENEDICTUS is broken by the liturgically dictated repeat of the OSANNA. There should be no real pause between the two movements, so that a direct connection might emphasize both the unity of the OSANNA-BENEDICTUS-OSANNA and the contrasts between the individual movements.

AGNUS DEI and DONA NOBIS PACEM

The last two movements are bound together by their texts. The three cries of *Agnus Dei, qui tollis peccata mundi* ("Lamb of God, who takes away the sins of the world"), are followed twice by the plea, *miserere nobis* ("have mercy on us"), and in the final movement, by *dona nobis pacem* ("grant us peace").

Bach set the first two sections of the text as an alto aria; the third, he set as the closing chorus. It is thus noteworthy that while the text of the aria is internally complete, the DONA NOBIS PACEM lacks the preceding *Agnus Dei, qui tollis peccata mundi*. The most basic reason for this lies in the structure of the final chorus as a parody of the GRATIAS AGIMUS TIBI. In order to accommodate the new text, Bach made some revisions to the movement as it appears in the *GLORIA*, but these left no room for the inclusion of the missing words. Too, the D-major key of the movement would have been inconsistent with the expression of that text. It could be argued from the proportions of the forty-nine measure aria, however, that Bach did not simply omit the third *Agnus Dei, qui tollis peccata mundi*. He formulated the first two prayers of the text in two equally long sections of twenty-two measures each. The identical length of these sections is particularly striking, since the instrumental introduction in the first case comprises eight measures, but in the second, it consists of only four. Five measures remain at the end of the aria. These do not possess the chracter of a postlude; rather, like the preceding instrumental sections, they function as an introduction.

In this instrumental passage, which differs sharply from the others (we shall discuss this when we come to the aria), it seems as if Bach formulated the third *Agnus Dei* in the instruments alone, completing it with the D-major setting of the DONA NOBIS PACEM.

AGNUS DEI

The fact that the AGNUS DEI is another revision of a cantata movement demonstrates once again that Bach did not parody earlier compositions merely as an expedient way out of a momentary predicament. Rather, here, in the greater context of the complete work, the parody produces for the first time the full development of the earlier thematic material. In the instrumental introduction to the aria on which the AGNUS DEI is based—*Ach bleibe doch, mein liebstes Leben, ach fliehe nicht so bald von mir* ("Ah, My Dearest Life, Flee Not So Soon from Me") from the "Ascension Oratorio" (BWV 11)—one can see clearly two allusions to the subject of the KYRIE ELEISON I fugue. In the second measure of both pieces, the tonic note is surrounded by chromatic half steps (arrows in ex. 144a). Then, in the third and fourth measures of the violin part to the aria, there is a clear motivic relationship between the sequential, slurred eighths and the corresponding motive in the first two bars of the KYRIE ELEISON I fugue (boxes in ex. 144a). Perhaps Bach selected this aria as the basis for his AGNUS DEI precisely because of this motivic and therefore expressive relationship with the fugue subject of the KYRIE ELEISON I. For the instrumental introduction to the AGNUS DEI, he omitted the restless thirty-second notes in the second measure of the model and provided a smooth connection between the two portions of the theme by means of the continuous eighth-note rhythm of the continuo in m. 5 (ex. 144b).

Ex. 144

Despite the motivic connection between the two movements, in the AGNUS DEI Bach progressively moves away from the model of the cantata movement. The dominant expressive quality of the aria is its great tranquility. This is ensured by the constant walking eighths of the continuo that appear, punctuated by rests, in nearly every bar save those at the end. Over the background of this writing for the continuo, the composition is constructed largely upon imitation. It is as if the text expressed by the voice is repeated meditatively by the instruments. The result is a great deal of canonic imitation (ex. 145) as well as the spinning

146

The shaping of the aria must seek to make equally clear the meditative and expressive components of the movement. The AGNUS DEI must therefore be characterized by both a slow tempo and a restraint in terms of dynamics. But though the dynamic scheme must not shy away from a genuine pianissimo in the fermata measure, it must also bring out the structurally dictated intensification in the next section of the movement. The linear tension that is obvious in the vocal writing must likewise characterize the shaping of the instrumental obbligato part. The obscurity that Bach so clearly desired for the closing ritornello is best achieved through a deliberate avoidance of any intensification. The resulting restraint serves as a point of departure for the final movement of the Mass.

DONA NOBIS PACEM

In the composition of the DONA NOBIS PACEM, Bach used the music of the GRATIAS AGIMUS TIBI. He thus deliberately rejected the possibility of concluding the Mass with a newly composed movement. In the discussion of the reasoning behind Bach's use of the choral movement from cantata 29 as the basis for the GRATIAS AGIMUS TIBI, it was shown that the messages of the cantata text and the Mass text were essentially identical. Bach's use of the music from a movement that he had already employed twice for the expression of thanks and praise invests the DONA NOBIS PACEM with a clear and precise meaning. The concern here is not with the suppliant prayer for God's mercy, but rather, with the praise of God and the acceptance of His promised peace, liberated from the tribulation of the preceding *miserere nobis*.

The double-fugue construction that was originally devised for cantata 29 and then adopted into the GRATIAS AGIMUS TIBI, is used here for the deliberate emphasis of different words for the text in each of the two fugue subjects. In the first subject the main stress is unmistakably upon the word *pacem*, which is even repeated (ex. 151a). The transposition of words in the second subject leads to the emphasis of the word *dona* (ex. 151b).

Ex. 151

Do - na - no - bis pa - cem, pa - cem,   pa - cem do - - - - - na no - bis

With these two subjects, Bach builds the double fugue the same way as he did in the cantata movement and the GRATIAS AGIMUS TIBI.

It is essential to the performance of this movement to establish continuity with the preceding AGNUS DEI, and to begin the DONA NOBIS PACEM immediately after the notated rest. An accent-free pianissimo at the beginning of the DONA NOBIS PACEM, corresponding to the restrained close of the AGNUS DEI, will reinforce the unity of the two movements. Then, as the tension of the plea for mercy progressively dissolves, and the setting constantly grows in intensity, the conclusion, with the trumpets radiating above, becomes a symbol of the majesty of God's peace (ex. 152).

THE TEXT OF THE MASS

KYRIE

Kyrie eleison.	Lord, have mercy.
Christe eleison.	Christ, have mercy.
Kyrie eleison.	Lord, have mercy.

GLORIA

Gloria in excelsis Deo,
Glory to God in the highest,

et in terra pax
hominibus bonae voluntatis.
and on earth peace
to men of good will.

Laudamus te, benedicimus te,
adoramus te, glorificamus te,
We praise You, we bless You,
we worship you, we glorify you,

gratias agimus tibi
propter magnam gloriam tuam:
we thank You
for Your great glory:

Domine Deus, Rex coelestis,
Deus Pater omnipotens.
Domine Fili unigenite, Jesu Christe
[Bach adds the word *altissime*];
Domine Deus,
Agnus Dei, Filius Patris:
O Lord God, King of heaven,
God the Father Almighty.
O Lord Jesus Christ, the only-begotten Son
[high above all];
O Lord God
Lamb of God, Son of the Father:

qui tollis peccata mundi,
miserere nobis;
qui tollis peccata mundi,
suscipe deprecationem nostram;
qui sedes ad dexteram Patris,
miserere nobis.
who takes away the sins of the world,
have mercy on us;
who takes away the sins of the world,
give ear to our prayer;
who sits at the right hand of the Father,
have mercy on us.

Quoniam tu solus Sanctus,
tu solus Dominus,
tu solus altissimus:
Jesu Christe,
For You alone are holy,
You alone are the Lord,
You alone are high above all:
Jesus Christ,

cum Sancto Spiritu
in gloria Dei Patris. Amen.
with the Holy Spirit
in the glory of God the Father. Amen.

SYMBOLUM NICENUM (CREDO)

Credo in unum Deum,	I believe in one God,
Patrem omnipotentem,	the Father almighty,
factorem coeli et terrae,	maker of heaven and earth,
visibilium omnium et invisibilium.	and of all things visible and invisible.
Et in unum Dominum Jesum Christum,	And in one Lord Jesus Christ,
Filium Dei unigenitum,	the only-begotten Son of God,
et ex Patre natum ante omnia saecula.	born of the Father before all ages.
Deum de Deo, lumen de lumine,	God of God, light of light,
Deum verum de Deo vero.	true God of true God.
Genitum, non factum,	Begotten, not made,
consubstantialem Patri,	being of one substance with the Father,
per quem omnia facta sunt.	by whom all things were made.
Qui propter nos homines	Who for us men
et propter nostram salutem	and for our salvation
descendit de coelis.	came down from heaven.
Et incarnatus est	And was incarnate
de Spiritu Sancto	by the Holy Spirit
ex Maria Virgine	of the Virgin Mary
et homo factus est.	and was made man.
Crucifixus etiam pro nobis:	He was crucified also for us:
sub Pontio Pilato	under Pontius Pilate
passus et sepultus est.	He suffered and was buried.
Et resurrexit tertia die,	And the third day He rose again,
secundum scripturas.	according to the scriptures.
Et ascendit in coelum: sedet	And He ascended into heaven:
ad dexteram [Bach adds the word *Dei*]	he sits at the right hand of [God]
Patris.	the Father.
Et iterum venturus est cum gloria	And He shall come again with glory
judicare vivos et mortuos:	to judge both the living and the dead:
cujus regni non erit finis.	of His kingdom there shall be no end.
Et in Spiritum Sanctum,	And in the Holy Spirit,
Dominum et vivificantem,	the Lord and giver of life,
qui cum Patre Filioque procedit,	who proceeds from the Father and the Son,
qui cum Patre et Filio	who together with the Father and the Son
simul adoratur et conglorificatur:	is worshipped and glorified:
qui locutus est per prophetas.	who spoke by the prophets.
Et unam sanctam catholicam	And in one holy catholic
et apostolicam ecclesiam.	and apostolic church.

Confiteor unum baptisma	I confess one baptism
in remissionem peccatorum	for the remission of sins
et expecto resurrectionem mortuorum	and I look for the resurrection of the dead
et vitam venturi saeculi.	and the life of the world to come.
Amen.	Amen.

SANCTUS

Sanctus, sanctus, sanctus	Holy, holy, holy
Dominus Deus sabaoth:	Lord God of hosts:
pleni sunt coeli et terra	heaven and earth are full
gloria Ejus.	of Your glory.

OSANNA-BENEDICTUS-OSANNA

Osanna in excelsis.	Hosanna in the highest!
Benedictus qui venit	Blessed is He who comes
in nomine Domini.	in the name of the Lord.
Osanna in excelsis.	Hosanna in the highest!

AGNUS DEI-DONA NOBIS PACEM

Agnus Dei,	Lamb of God,
qui tollis peccata mundi,	who takes away the sins of the world,
miserere nobis.	have mercy on us.
Agnus Dei,	Lamb of God,
qui tollis peccata mundi,	who takes away the sins of the world,
miserere nobis.	have mercy on us.
[Bach omits the words *Agnus Dei, qui tollis peccata mundi,*]	[Lamb of God, who takes away the sins of the world,]
dona nobis pacem.	grant us peace.

(Translation adapted from The Cathedral Daily Missal [St. Paul: E.M. Lohmann], 1961.)

FOOTNOTES

[1]Georg von Dadelsen, *Beiträge zur Chronologie der Werke Johann Sebastian Bachs* [Contributions to the chronology of the works of Johann Sebastian Bach], *Tübinger Bach Studien*, vols. 4/5 (Trossingen, 1958). "*Exkurs über die h-moll Messe*" [Essay on the B-Minor Mass], in *Johann Sebastian Bach*, ed. Walter Blankenburg, *Wege der Forschung*, vol. 170 (Darmstadt, 1970), pp. 334-352.

[2]Walter Blankenburg, *Einführung in h-moll Messe* [Introduction to the B-Minor Mass], third, revised edition (Kassel: Bärenreiter, 1974), with extensive bibliography.

[3]Gerhard Herz, *Der lombardische Rhythmus im* Domine Deus *der h-moll Messe J.S. Bachs* [Lombardic rhythm in the *Domine Deus* from J.S. Bach's B-Minor Mass], *Bach Jahrbuch*, vol. 60 (Berlin: Evangelische Verlagsanstalt, 1974), pp. 90-97. Frederick Neumann believes that the lombardic rhythm at the beginning of the first-flute part was not meant to denote the written rhythm; rather, that it was intended to signal the French flutist at the Dresden Court *not* to play the passage as *notes inégales*. Neumann does not address the presence of lombardic rhythm in the other parts. See Frederick Neumann, "The Overdotting Syndrome: Anatomy of a Delusion," *Musical Quarterly*, July, 1981, p. 305. For a discussion of this question with regard to the works of Bach in general, see Gerhard Herz, *Der lombardische Rhythmus in Bachs Vocalschaffen* [Lombardic rhythm in Bach's vocal works], *Bach Jahrbuch*, vol. 64 (Berlin: Evangelische Verlagsanstalt, 1978), pp. 148-180.

OTHER PRESTIGE RELEASES

1. Erik Routley, CHRISTIAN HYMNS: A CASSETTE SERIES. $59.95

2. Richard Evans, MUSIC ADMINISTRATION: AN ANNOTATED BIBLIOGRAPHY. $10.00

3. Erik Routley, CHRISTIAN HYMNS OBSERVED: WHEN IN OUR MUSIC GOD IS GLORIFIED. $9.95

4. William Hipp, EVALUATING MUSIC FACULTY. $10.00

5. Ray Robinson, KRZYSZTOF PENDERECKI: A GUIDE TO HIS WORKS. $7.95

6. Erik Routley, THE DIVINE FORMULA. $11.95

7. Erik Routley, A SHORT HISTORY OF ENGLISH CHURCH MUSIC. $9.95

Order From:
Prestige Publications, Inc.
P.O. Box 2157
Princeton, New Jersey 08540